THE COMPLETE LYRICS OF FACE TO FACE AND OTHERS (1990–2020)

TREVER KEITH

INCLUDING ILLUSTRATIONS BY RAY TATTOOED BOY
AND A NEW FOREWORD BY RICH EGAN

RARE BIRD
Los Angeles, California

THIS IS A GENUINE RARE BIRD BOOK

Rare Bird Books
6044 North Figueroa Street
Los Angeles, CA 90042
rarebirdbooks.com

FIRST HARDCOVER EDITION

For more information, address:
Rare Bird Books Subsidiary Rights Department
6044 North Figueroa Street
Los Angeles, CA 90042

Set in Georgia
Printed in the United States

10 9 8 7 6 5 4 3 2 1

Publisher's Cataloging-in-Publication Data available upon request.

FOREWORD

"I want to know...Do these words mean anything?"

WORDS ARE FUNNY THINGS. What is life defining to one set of ears can be meaningless filler to another.

Punk rock has an even more conflicted relationship with words. It's one of those riddles like the tree falling in a forest with no one to hear it...if a punk rock song doesn't have lyrics, is it a punk rock song?

I would argue that such a thing does not exist. However, if your definition of punk rock is a soundtrack for running in circles and smashing into other sweaty revelers for ninety minutes then, sure, who needs lyrics? And for that matter, who needs punk rock?

The answer, of course, is you do (which is why you are holding this book). I do. In a perfect world, everyone would.

The world would be a better place if the genres' best were celebrated as the great writers of the past were. Why don't we speak of Joe Strummer, Bill Stevenson, Blake Schwarzenbach, and Trever Keith the same way we talk about Jack Kerouac, Allen Ginsberg, and William Burroughs? All of them moved a culture, all of them shook the status quo, all of them changed lives with their words. Are punk rock poets penalized for having distorted guitars behind their words instead of bongo drums?

If you can pull the words away from the music and they stand on their own as solitary works that inspire, enlighten and run you through every emotion imaginable, that's great literature—and that should be celebrated.

Trever Keith is one of the genres' best lyricists. His words aren't highfalutin. They are not overtly political. They are never wacky and he doesn't write broken-hearted love songs. What Trever does better than anyone is write songs for the collective "we." For thirty years, he has managed to capture what it means it means to struggle, win, lose, rise up, and do it all over again. He puts words to those voices in our heads, that tell us we can't...we won't...we can...and we will. His songs are triumphant without ever being bombastic. He makes us believe without ever preaching. His lyrics have gotten so many of us through so much.

Trever Keith can say more in two minutes and forty-five seconds than most songwriters can in an entire album. And he does it all wrapped in melodies and hooks that make the most jaded of critics sing along (admit it, you're humming "Blind" right now, aren't you?). The *face to face* albums aren't platinum. They are just the best. Their live shows don't sell out arenas, they are just better than everyone else's. Trever Keith is not lauded as the everyman's poet laureate. He just is.

—Rich Egan, Vagrant Records

INTRODUCTION

WRITING IS PROBLEMATIC FOR me. I have a love/hate relationship with it. This is partly because I love how writing allows connections with others through the communication of thoughts and emotions, but it's for the same reason I hate it. I hate it because, most of the time, it is difficult for me to share thoughts and emotions that are personal. The problem is, in my mind, I think the only way to write something compelling is to reveal something personal. Then my issue becomes how to give just enough of myself in the lyrics to make them compelling without completely giving myself away. This is usually the goal for me, to find that happy medium in sharing my own personal thoughts that are important to me, and hope that others will find it compelling. When it works, there is no greater feeling than the connections made with others through communicating emotions and ideas through lyrics and music. When it doesn't work... well, let's just say it far less gratifying.

I started writing lyrics in my teens. They were pretty bad. I'm grateful that they're likely obscure enough now that know one else will ever see them. They were full of rock n roll cliches at first, then they became far too serious, mirroring my musical tastes at the time from cheesy hair metal bands to more prog rock stuff like Iron Maiden, etc. Thankfully, by the time *face to face* was starting up I had already outgrown my propensity for writing either vapid rock n roll lyrics or overwrought metal epics.

When I look back at the early lyrics for our debut album *Don't Turn Away,* I can, of course, find flaws because I was young and struggling to find an identity and not very accomplished at songwriting. As a writer, *face to face* was the start of me finding a lyrical stride. I'm probably still not very accomplished at songwriting, but I am experienced. I think what was strong about those early lyrics is their simplicity. When I look back at them now as I gather all of the lyrics together of the past thirty years for this book, I think I'm finding meaning that I may not have known existed back then. Sometimes they miss the mark, but I feel like many of these lyrics have held up pretty well throughout the years. Overall, many of these lyrics contain themes of overcoming obstacles that prevent us from self-fulfillment and happiness with the intent that if we can become better, we can do better by people around us. I guess that sounds a bit lofty for punk rock songs, but through my lyrics I have and still do ultimately want to communicate positivity.

I have decided to arrange this book in alphabetical order rather than in chronological order. This will definitely obscure the reader's ability to see my "growth" as a writer, and that's partly why I did it. I am egotistical like the rest of you, and I don't really like putting a spotlight on my weaknesses. I hope it also provides variety as you read this book, because there are songs next to each other which were written decades apart from each other. This should provide an interesting juxtaposition of my headspace as a twenty-something, and now as a fifty-something. In the end, creating music and lyrics for me has always been about making emotional connections and I sincerely hope this book does just that.

—Trever Keith

1,000 X

I've tried to ask the question
must be a million answers thatjust aren't there
You try to find yourself
I'll try to live my life
I just don't care

Take a look at your life
Tell me can you say you've done no wrong?
Ask yourself the question
Do you realize where you belong?

I've been down
I've been out
I've been there

I've been down this road a thousand times
Nothing ever looks the same
it seems to me
There's something more
that I might never see

I've been down
I've been out
I've been there

I've been down this road a thousand times
Nothing ever looks the same
it seems to me
There's something more
that I might never see

There's something more
that I might never see

1-2-3 DROP

You can't stay
used it up
You give 'em everything
they say it's not enough
Hold up your head
keep it up
No use sittin' 'round
waiting for the other shoe

1-2-3 drop!

No one will cry when they are dead
I hope they choke on every single word they said
to pay for every drop of blood that's shed
We'll all be alright when the walls come crumbling down

Bills to paypiling up
You work a little harder
but you're so fed up
Deep in a hole
looking up
No use sittin' 'round
waiting for the other shoe

1-2-3 drop!

No one will cry when they are dead
I hope they choke on every single word they said
to pay for every drop of blood that's shed
We'll all be alright when thewalls come crumbling down

1-2-3 drop!

14 HOURS

14 hours to go
and the waiting's almost done
When I get back home
you're going to be the only one

Staring at the lights or staring at the sun
Everyday another fight or ill to overcome

Another day, another place
Forgot the name but not the face
I've been away for too long to remember

14 hours to go
and the waiting's almost done
When I get back home
you're going to be the only one

Suspended animation, countdown has begun
Hurry up and wait
for all of the things that must be done

It doesn't matter what state I'm in
They've all been waiting so let's begin
I know that when I'm back
I'm going to miss it

14 hours to go
and the waiting's almost done
When I get back home
you're going to be the only one

A MISS IS AS GOOD AS A MILE

You pretend like you're alright
In somebody else's life
hiding in the chaos and disarray

Someday you'll put up a fight
Someday soon you'll make it right
"Someday" is drifting far away

Keep on saying it in your mind
Keep your head up you'll be fine
"Narrow is the path but wide the gates"

But if you shrink and try to hide
Fading away by your design
You'll never know anyone anyway

I meant to call you, by the way...

A miss is as good as a mile
I think you've got the hang of it
You've been at it a while
A miss is as good as a mile
I'm sure you'll make the best of it
said with a crooked smile

You pretend like you're alright
In somebody else's life
hiding in the chaos and disarray

But if you shrink and try to hide
Fading away by your design
You'll never know anyone anyway

I meant to call you, by the way...

A WOLF IN SHEEP'S CLOTHING

You've got your reputation
I've got anonymity
I've got my self-respect you can't take that from me
You've got to protect your interests
You've got your enemies
I've got a hundred reasonsto expose your treachery

There is no happy ending
Only what remains to be

I want an explanation
I want an apology
You ruined everything
You tried to run away but you can't
I want to hear the answer
I want the opportunity
You wasted so much time
You tried to run away but you can't

You had your way of speaking
I was full of naivete
We had a common interest
and a trust based on a need
I've got my own ideas
I've got my integrity
You've got your binding contracts
You've got your misery

There is no happy ending
Only what remains to be

I want an explanation
I want an apology

You ruined everything
You tried to run away but you can't
I want to hear the answer
I want the opportunity
You wasted so much time
You tried to run away but you can't

Your power and position
Your hunger and your greed
Walk on the backs of others
toward the goals you will achieve

I want an explanation
I want an apology
You ruined everything
You tried to run away but you can't
I want to hear the answer
I want the opportunity
You wasted so much time
You tried to run away but you can't

There is no happy ending

Only what remains to be

X-RAY
VISION

A-OK

You think that I'm invincible
It's going to pull me down
pull me down
You think that I'm invisible
It's going to pull me down
to somewhere I don't want to go
It's okay

You think I'm indestructible
It's going to pull me down
pull me down
You think that I'm a miracle
It's going to pull me down
to somewhere I don't want to go
It's okay

I don't know what you want from me
But it's probably already gone
I don't care what you think of me
Your opinion means nothing at all

Don't say I'm okay
Don't say I'm okay
Don't say I'm okay
I'm not okay

Don't say I've not tried
Tried to do what's right
Now it's time to walk away

I don't know what you want from me
But it's probably already gone
I don't care what you think of me
Your opinion means nothing at all

Don't say I'm okay
Don't say I'm okay
Don't say I'm okay
I'm not okay

"A-OK" is one of the early *face to face* songs. It was written in the same time period (1992–1993) when we were still working out a sound for the band. Although this one was written during the *Don't Turn Away* era of the band, it did not appear on that record. Instead, a version of it was first released on an EP called Over it. The most recognizable and maybe what you might call the "official" version was released on our sophomore album *Big Choice*.

What I think makes these lyrics different from the rest of the songs I was writing at the time is that this was the first time I tried experimenting with writing vulnerable lyrics. These lyrics are about human weakness, which of course is universal even though it is sometimes a difficult thing to admit especially in the backdrop of the punk rock music style which is usually aggressive and visceral. I think the music is definitely consistent with punk rock/hardcore in it's spirit, but the lyrics are about a feeling of desperation and exhaustion. This song to me is about outside forces putting pressure on you to deliver something you don't have or to be someone that you are not. But it's not only about external pressure, it's about the pressure we place on ourselves to meet the perceived expectations of the people around us.

Even though this one is very early in our career, it remains one of my favorites musically and lyrically because even after years of performing this song, I think it has aged well. It remains relevant and it still has personal meaning for me because the theme is timeless. You never grow out of it.

ABSOLUTION

It's not as easy getting numb
Deny the thing that you've become
You'll be sorry
for the things you've said and done

Take a good look at yourself
You're just like everybody else
We make excuses for the things we can't outrun

If everything I've ever done was wrong
then thanks to you for pointing out
my glaring and my smallest
imperfections

Let this be a lesson
I was only trying to set things right
There's no absolution
There is only will and means
selling faith to whoever will buy

I guess it's easier for some
to just ignore this droning hum
but you'll be sorry
for the things you've said and done

The true believers tell themselves
they're not like anybody else
Do you believe that you've been true with anyone?

If everything I've ever done was wrong
then thanks to you for pointing out
my glaring and my smallest
imperfections

Let this be a lesson
I was only trying to set things right
There's no absolution
There is only will and means
selling faith to whoever will buy

Maybe I'm uncomfortable
Maybe this got old
Impatient and insufferable
Feels like everything is wrong

ACROSS STATE LINES

There's fear in everyone
You can manipulate it
Just pull the strings and watch the show

Bright lights as we go by
they fade into darkness
winding down this unknown road

You wouldn't be caught dead
in something less than stylish
And you won't be going home again

We're going to run it all night
Running across state lines
And I don't want this to end
We're going to run it all night

A chance for everyone
They really still believe it
Just bait your hook and tug the line

The night sky hangs above
And under a veil of secrets
there's a greater truth we can't deny

You wouldn't be caught dead
in something less than stylish
And you won't be going home again

We're going to run it all night
Running across state lines
And I don't want this to end
We're going to run it all night

ALL FOR NOTHING

I have given up the demons
I've made up a hundred reasons
I have turned my backon everything I knew

I have justified my actions
Been denied the satisfaction
I've believed and I have put away the truth

All to be with you

I have lost the inhibitions
I have felt a deep contrition
And I've realized there's still so much to do

I was lost inside my own lies
I fell victim and I thought I'd
never find the strength
to do what I must do

All to be with you

I've been inside Hell and out of
I've done things I'm less than proud of
I have only ever tried to get to you

I've lost everything and still I've
never given up until I
either die
or I will make it back to you

All to be with you

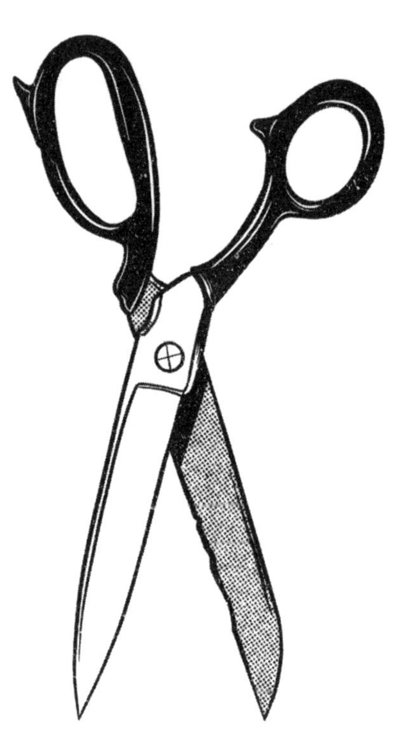

AND SO IT GOES

And so it goes
pretend like nobody knows
I keep it close
hold on for dear life

So here we are
we struggled to get this far
The truth hit the mark
but I never lied

I take a breath, the knife twists
but doesn't hurt like before
Been with me so long
it's something I couldn't ignore
Can't forget what it's here for

You call it what you want it doesn't change a thing
We're all made of flesh and bone just the same
Go on point the finger and try and place the blame
I'm made up of flesh and bone just the same

And so it goes
ahead but not even close
I used the wrong voice
but I never lied

I take a breath the knife twists
but doesn't hurt like before
Been with me so long
it's something I couldn't ignore
Can't forget what it's here for

You call it what you want it doesn't change a thing
We're all made of flesh and bone just the same
Go on point the finger and try and place the blame
I'm made up of flesh and bone just the same

So what's left to say
when so many questions are raised?
If nothing can change then what am I fighting for?
I did my best
I never gave anything less
and I'll never rest
it's something you can't ignore

I take a breath the knife twists
but doesn't hurt like before
Been with me so long
it's something I couldn't ignore
Can't forget what it's here for

You call it what you want it doesn't change a thing
We're all made of flesh and bone just the same
Go on point the finger and try and place the blame
I'm made up of flesh and bone just the same

ANONYMOUS

It's been a while since I've been back
You barely noticed I was gone
You did a number on yourself
You let it go for far too long

I tried to take a break from this
couldn't stay away too long
Thought I could make the best of it
I knew that I was wrong
Where do we belong?

So you're lonely?
you've only just begun to feel
much of anything
I'm sorry I ever wanted
anyone to know my name

You said that I'm the one to blame
I know that nothing's going to change
But if you're honest with yourself
you know that everyone's the same

I tried to take a break from this
couldn't stay away too long
Thought I could make the best of it
I knew that I was wrong
Where do we belong?

So you're lonely?
you've only just begun to feel
much of anything
I'm sorry I ever wanted
anyone to know my name

So much for being clever
So much for thinking
I could come back to the same placewhere I started
from
Now it's all gone
Tell me where you think that we belong

So you're lonely?
you've only just begun to feel
much of anythingI'm sorry
I'm sorry I ever wanted
anyone to know my name

"Anonymous" is from our tenth studio album *No Way Out But Through*. This record was an interesting one to make because *face to face* had been doing a lot of touring all the way and up through the end of 2019. In January of 2020, Scott and I literally woodshedded to write new material for the record. By literally I mean we wrote everything in a sort of wooden cabin type thing that I had put myself in to inspire some creativity. It turned out to be a very good thing because in a matter of days we had written all of the material for the record. In March we went into the studio to record and after the second day had to shut down production because of COVID 19. We had only managed to capture bass and drum performances.

Making the record continued to be a decidedly different experience as we recorded vocals and guitars while keeping masks and social distancing in place at one studio and then p[proceeded to record material from our home studios. This was a Covid 19 year record but since the material was written prior to any mention of the pandemic, the songs aren't about Covid 19.

"Anonymous" was originally going to be called Cancel Culture, but I felt that the working title was a bit too direct and that the intention might be misunderstood. The song's theme changed slightly with the new title. It is at it's core a relationship song. More specifically a relationship in decline. The reasons for the decline aren't important but what is important is the theme of allowing yourself to become vulnerable only to regret that you did. It's a song about how it is safe to be anonymous when know one knows you but "wanting someone to know your name" puts you at risk of judgement and harm.

ANOTHER DIVERSION

I guess I'm just like everyone
Too buried in the middle of this static
We want the truth
apart from everyone
along with all of the fabrications in it

But we're so self-absorbed
It doesn't seem to make a difference
unless we get our faces pushed in it

So come on everyone
let's believe in someone else
to give us what we want

I hope I'm not the only one
who thinks it's probably nothing more than static
We need to feel
like part of something more
to justify the reason that we're in it

But we're so self-absorbed
It doesn't seem to make a difference
unless we get our faces shoved in it

So come on everyone let's believe in someone else
to give us what we want

So come on everyone let's believe in someone else
to give us what we want

ANYBODY LISTENING?

You're calling out and no one pays attention
Looks like everything is still the same
It's nothing we can change

You're calling out and no one pays attention
Looks like everything is still the same
It's nothing we can change

Charity is an illusion
No one really owns a thing
Complication and confusion
To ease your suffering and pain

You're calling out
And no one pays attention
Looks like everything is still the same
It's nothing we can change

You're calling out and no one pays attention
Looks like everything is still the sameI
t's nothing we can change

Charity is an illusion
No one really owns a thing
Complication and confusion
To ease your suffering and pain
You're calling out

(A)PATHETIC

It feels like there's nothing I can do
It feels like there's nothing left to do

Always feels like I must
WAIT
just a while
because
"anything worth having is worth the wait"
So it seems
that this waiting has left us somewhere in-between

It feels like there's nothing I can do
It feels like there's nothing left to do

Blind ambition is overrated
Apathetic, bored, and jaded now

You forget something
I wanted to be left alone

You forget something
I wanted to be left alone

You forget something
I wanted to be left alone

You forget something
I wanted to be left alone

ARE YOU UNCOMFORTABLE?

Has there ever been a time you'd forgotten who you
were?
Are you not culpable?
The moment you decidean impossible return
Are you uncomfortable?

Steady

A misdirected truth
you've accepted what you've learned
It's so predictable
An aching deep inside you pretended wasn't there
Are you uncomfortable?

Steady

Filter through desire
and suppress the willing urge
Are you emotional?
Forget you're civilized
and become what you once were
Are you uncomfortable?

Steady

The moment you decide
an impossible return
It's so predictable
Forget you're civilized
and become what you once were
Are you uncomfortable?

Steady

BENT BUT NOT BROKEN

Why are we still so surprised
every time we buy the lie?
Why don't we pursue the truth
even when it's hard to do?

And all we want is to believe
It's okay if we're slightly deceived
Maybe we're missing the pointthat we're listening
to liars and thieves

You're bent but you just won't break
Some things will never change

Why are we so slow to say
they've figured out another way?
Why are we so quick to judge
anyone who's not like us?

And all we want is to believe
It's okay if we're slightly deceived
Maybe we're missing the pointthat we're listening
To liars and thieves

You're bent but you just won't break
Some things will never change

You said that you would never be in lockstep
walking with the rest of them
I barely recognize if there is anything left of you
and I want something more

You're bent but you just won't break
Some things will never change

BEST DEFENSE

You haven't heard a word of what I said
I'd give anything
to get inside your head
You act as if there's nothing left to say
I guess everything
is easier that way
I know that you don't want to think about it anyway

I won't let you hide from this
Even with your best defense
you can't deny the way you feel about me

I know you think about it all of time
But there's nothing left
to make you change your mind
I know you think you're doing what is right
But you're acting on
frustration out of spite
And I don't want to say another word to start a fight

I won't let you hide from this
Even with your best defense
you can't deny the way you feel about me

And if you're so convinced
that we're so wrong
You're still standing here
where you've been all along
It doesn't make much differencewhere we think that
we belong

I won't let you hide from this
Even with your best defense
you can't deny the way you feel about me

BIG CHOICE

Big lies! Surprise!
You've thought of everything
It builds your character you know
No way? Okay
So what's the price you pay?
Too late to realize you're broke

Do you think that everything worked out?
It's good to see you've finally made it
Can't you see you're lying to yourself?

But this was all your choice
Do you think it makes a difference now?
But this was all your choice and
it's good to see it hasn't changed you

You've tried,Denied!
Can't win at everything
It's building character you know
Don't wait...too late
You've got a choice to make
It's time to do what you've been told

Do you think that everything worked out?
It's good to see you've finally made it
Can't you see you're lying to yourself?

But this was all your choice
Do you think it makes a difference now?
But this was all your choice and it's good to see it hasn't
changed you

But this was all your choice
Do you think it makes a difference now?
But this was all your choice and nothing's changed you
But this was all your choice

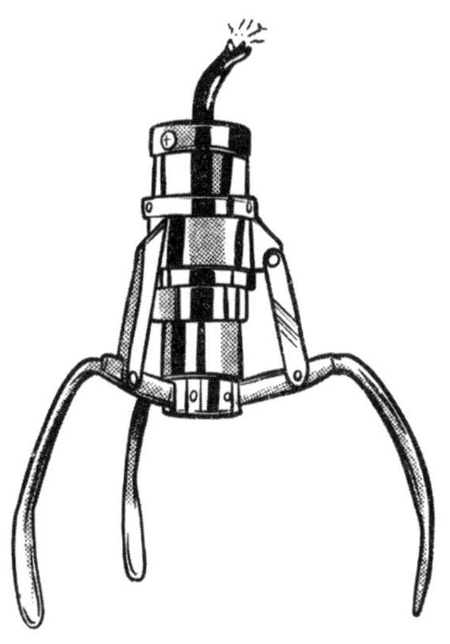

BILL OF GOODS

Try to convince you that you can't live without one
Hey look around man everybody's got one!
So hurry up and get your dollar bills together
They're going to try and get yousomething even better

You're not so sure but you heard it's great
You get there first so you won't be late
Everybody else will have to wait in line

I overestimated you
you knew that I probably would
We're so predictable
and we've been sold a bill of goods

You want a choice
Want to make your own decisions
You want to make up the rules and the provisions

And everything is going to be so great
when you're the latest keeper at the gate
Everybody else will have to wait in line

I overestimated you
you knew that I probably would
We're so predictable
and we've been sold a bill of goods

Try to convince you that you can't live without one
Hey look around man everybody's got one!
So hurry upget your dollar bills together
They're going to try and get yousomething even better

BLACK EYE SPECIALIST

You really made a mess of it
This one takes the cake
Self-loathing's got the best of you
There's almost nothing left to hate

I'm the black eye specialist
Make the best of you
Cover up the "accident"
Make you good as new

I think I speak for everyone
We don't hate you
We create you
This is not an intervention
but there's a price to pay
You'll have to live with yourself

It isn't like you asked for it
You're just about to break
It isn't indefensible
there's only so much you can can take

I'm the black eye specialist
Make the best of you
Cover up the "accident"
Make you good as new

I think I speak for everyone
We don't hate you
We create you
This is not an intervention
but there's a price to pay
You'll have to live with yourself

BLANKED OUT

So tell me where we go from here?
and is is better to be full of fear
than to be hateful? I don't know
Is there something better out there?

I thought that I'd remember
What you said to me
What you said to me

I swear I can't remember
What you said to me
What you said to me

I tried to reach you
but I think you've blanked me out

So tell me what I want to hear
Pull up a chair and bend my ear
I'll hang on every syllable
There's nothing better out there

I thought that I'd remember
What you said to me
What you said to me

I swear I can't remember
What you said to me
What you said to me

It might be too late
feels like you've blanked me outI tried to reach you
but I think you've blanked me out

BLEEDING OUT

If all of this and all of that means nothing
It's such a waste of time
Indifferent, unkind
We pride ourselves in knowing that we're better
than everyone like you
Which one then am I?

I could never care enough
I could never give enough
I could never bleed enough to please you
You need everything

A give and take through waking hours of dreaming
Building confidence
Preparing for the worst
So off we go intent on getting somewhere
Anywhere but here
As long as you're there first

I could never care enough
I could never give enough
I could never bleed enough to please you
You need everything

Fill it up until it's overflowing
So full that you can't breathe
Suffocate the dream
It's not enough to satisfy the aching
And so relentlessly devouring everything

I could never care enough
I could never give enough
I could never bleed enough to please you
You need everything

BLIND

What if I'm right and you are wrong?
What if you knew it all along?
What if I figured out that I did not belong?

What if it always bothered me?
What if I never did believe?
Would it be wrong if I decided I should leave?

If I pretended I was blind
and struck it from my mind
would it still be there?
What if I'd do anything to make it seem all right?
It's alright

What if it's all inside my head?
What if those words were never said?
Would it be easier if I could just forget?

What if I didn't run away?
Could it be any other way?
Would it be wrong if I decided I should stay?

If I pretended I was blind
and struck it from my mind
would it still be there?
What if I'd do anything to make it seem all right?
It's alright

“Blind” is a song that almost didn’t make it on to our 1996 self-titled record. I remember writing it and really liking the song but I was worried it wouldn’t be “punk rock” enough for our audience. We rehearsed it a few times and everybody thought it was cool so we made it a part of our live set. We performed it on our Econolive Tour where we were really just testing the waters for all of the new songs that we had written for what would become our third album. I remember that at first the audiences seemed to just sort of slow down and stand there and listen to the song rather than react physically to it. Once we released it on our self-titled album and people became familiar with it, “Blind” became one of our most iconic tracks and a staple in the setlist.

This one has almost a lullaby style melody that is simple and immediate. I wanted the lyrics to fit with the very simple style of the music. I started with the idea for the first couple of lines and then I wondered if I could write an entire song that was a series of questions rather than statements. I put myself to the challenge and made a song of questions except for the reassuring statement at the end of every chorus “it’s alright” which is really meant to be your own inner voice convincing yourself of something you know not to be true. The lyrics are an exploration of something most of us have experienced either through our own behavior or we’ve seen it exhibited in others. We can sometimes purposefully choose not to see the things that are obvious and right in front of us. I suppose this is a kind of defense mechanism that shields us from things unpleasant or truths we do not want to acknowledge.

BLOOD AND ORANGES

We've all got our faith in superman
and we don't care how he gets it done
We want to wake up everyday
secure in knowing what we believe is true

We're all so ashamed
We must be to blame
for everything that's wrong

So why the weakness?
I don't know
And why the pretense when we know the truth?
It's just a matter of time

We all want our cake and eat it too
Then we feel ashamed for what we've done
We demand the knowledge and the truth
Behaving like we've been staring at the sun

We're all so ashamed
We must be to blame
For everything that's wrong

So why the weakness?
I don't know
And why the pretense when we know the truth?
It's just a matter of time

BLOOD IN THE WATER

What's your name?
I don't care and I don't think it means a thing anymore
It's still the same
Here you are for a minute with your foot out the door

And everybody wants
to take a little piece if they can
And you're no better than the rest
when it is someone else but you

It's like suddenly you're everybody's friend
And it's ending just as soon as it begins
It's like blood is in the water once again
You've been bleeding in this place for so long

Congratulations, you're the one!
Let's get to work there's so much to be done
You promised we could have our fun
Don't give them anything
or you'll have nothing left

What's the game?
Are you aware that you don't own a single thing
anymore?
It's a shame
I used to think that you were betterI can't tell anymore

And everybody tries
to take a little piece if they can
But you're no better than the rest
when they want someone else but you

It's like suddenly you're everybody's friend
And it's ending just as soon as it begins
It's like blood is in the water once again
You've been bleeding
in this place for so long

Congratulations, you're the one!
Let's get to work there's so much to be done
You promised we could have our fun
Don't give them anything
or you'll have nothing left

BOMBS AWAY

It's time for an intervention
It's time for a little truth
It's time for a revolution
Grab a torch gonna light the fuse

Had enough of the desperation
Had enough of the crooked views
Had enough and it's time for action 3-2-1
no time to lose

There comes a time
when you've got to make your stand
Bombs away
let the casualties be damned

We don't want your consideration
We don't want to be recognized
We don't want your procrastination
The time is now to get organized
Fall in line revolutionary
Fall in line, gonna win the war
Fall in line, you're another number
A call to arms now
1-2-3-4

There comes a time
when you've got to make your stand
Bombs away
let the casualties be damned

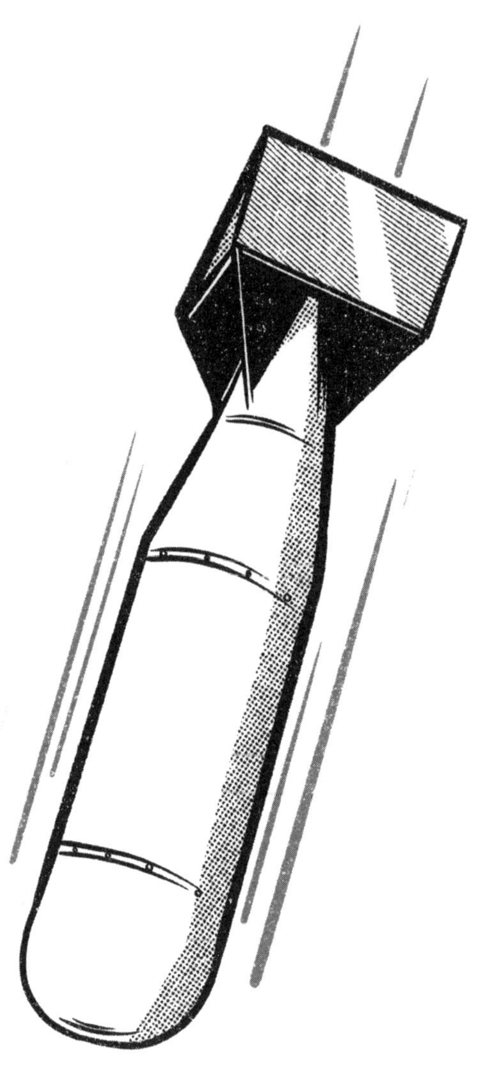

BOTTLE ROCKETS

I thought that I'd be strong enough for both of us
but you had given up
Is there anybody strong enough for you?
She said she's scared of waking up
to realize it's all been a mistake
But you didn't have to be afraid

You walked out on me
It doesn't really matter what you said
Because I've tried
To turn this water into wine
What she said

It doesn't have to be so hard to understand
The things that we should do
I know I've made it difficult for you
She said I couldn't give enough
to make her feel the way she wanted to
This doesn't have to be so hard

But you walked out on me
It doesn't really matter what you said
And I tried to turn this water into wine

What she said

It takes time
It's not that way
There are several different answers here
but you just walked away

What she said

THE BREAKS

You really think that you can make a difference?
You try and try to make this world a better place
No one can argue with your best intentions
But the more things change
the more they're gonna stay the same

Let me go on
Look around you nobody's watching
Let me go on
Something to say but nobody listens

You want more than you can take
Outreached your grasp and that's your first mistake
Lost everything and them's the breaks
Look in the mirror you ain't getting any younger

He's gonna show them there's nobody better
He's gonna try and take as much as he can take
No matter what, he's got to be the winner
There's no reward in life coming in second place

Let me go on
Look around you nobody's watching
Let me go on
Something to say but nobody listens

You want more than you can take
Outreached your grasp and that's your first mistake
Lost everything and them's the breaks
Look in the mirror you ain't getting any younger

BRIGHT LIGHTS GO DOWN

Bright lights go down
Bright lights go down
They say there'll come a day
when you better get ready for the breakdown
Until the bright lights go down

If you don't stand for something
you'll fall for anything
I remember when I said this
and I was full of it

I made it up
because it's what they say
I've had enough of people anyway
So let's get out
and burn this day down to the ground

Until the bright lights go down
Bright lights go down
They say there'll come a day
when you better get ready for the breakdown
Until the bright lights go down

No atheists in a foxhole?
You never had nothing to lose
Are you just when when it's convenient?
Climb aboard this ship of fools

There's nothing left
for you and I to say
You've done your best
it's gonna be okay
Forget the rest
of what you want to say and stay gold

Until the bright lights go down
Bright lights go down
They say there'll come a day
when you better get ready for the breakdown
Until the bright lights go down

BURDEN

You could say
I might find it difficult to show it on the outside
From far away
I should seem as ordinary
as would seem the truth
But all we find dishonesty and lies
It's hard to recognize the truth
And why can't I
discover what the reason is that I
know there's something left that I should prove?

I didn't mean to burden you
Is there something more to this?
I didn't mean to burden you
Is there something more to this?
Was it something I've already missed?

Peel away
the fear that I'm not good enough
to give back what I've taken
It's hard to say
the disappointment tends
to make the optimism fade
I'm still behind
and running out of time
It's nothing but a trite excuse
So why can't I
discover what the reason is that I
know there's something left that I should prove?

I didn't mean to burden you
Is there something more to this?
I didn't mean to burden you
Is there something more to this?
Was it something I've already missed?

BURNED

Burn!
Burn that expectation to the ground
Burn that stupid notion to a crisp
Burned by exploitation
felt the singe
My face is black with ashes

I don't care about
what you you want me to be today
because I just can't get it right
I don't care about anything
I'm just sick of the smell of this kerosene

Burn!
Burn those aspirations to the ground
burn that expectation to a crisp
burnt by implication
felt the singe
My face is black with ashes

I'm not sure about
how you want me to be right now
because I'm not here anyway
I don't want anything
I'm just sick of the price of this gasoline

Burn!
Burn that expectation to the ground
Burn that stupid notion to a crisp
Burned by exploitation
felt the singe
My face is black with ashes

CAN'T CHANGE THE WORLD

People say that it's impossible to fly
but you don't know what I'm thinking
Don't want to be just like the other hundred guys
You don't know what I'm thinking

Can't change the world?
You say it's crumbling all around you
and you're trying to get out

Can't change the world?
You say it's crumbling all around you
and you're trying to get out

People say that out of sight is out of mind
but you don't know what I'm thinking
Don't want to listen to the ignorance and lies
You don't know what I'm thinking

Can't change the world?
You say it's crumbling all around you
and you're trying to get out

Can't change the world?
You say it's crumbling all around you
and you're trying to get out

And isn't it ironic sometimes?
The things we take for granted are what we wanted
before we knew why
And isn't it the reason we try?
To make the excuse that it won't go the right way
before it's gone wrong

People say that it's impossible to fly
but you don't know what I'm thinking
Don't want to be just like the other hundred guys
You don't know what I'm thinking

COMING OUT OF NOWHERE

It's unfair unjustified
not for the lack of how you tried
Hits you coming out of nowhere

Are you happy with your life?
It's going well you're feeling fine
Hits you coming out of nowhere

Is it your money or your life?
A question you won't dignify?
Hits you coming out of nowhere

When you leave this all behind
how will we all remember you?
Hits you coming out of nowhere

I'm only this perception

It doesn't take a ton of bricks to shed a little light on this
I know I've made a few mistakes
and God I'm bound to make some more today

But I've made my bed so I'll lay in it
I'll take what I didn't get
Stay awake and try not to forget
It fades away

You square off focused on the prize
The struggle then you realize
Hits you coming out of nowhere

You don't believe and its alright
There's nothing you're supposed to do
Hits you coming out of nowhere

I'm only this perception

It doesn't take a ton of bricks to shed a little light on this
I know I've made a few mistakes
and God I'm bound to make some more today

But I've made my bed so I'll lay in it
I'll take what I didn't get
Stay awake and try not to forget
It fades away

COMPLICATED

You're never going to see what you like
You're never going to wake up and change your mind
You're never going to keep what you hold
You won't accomplish anything on your own

You can't have what you wanted
So make up your mind and come to your senses

You'll never win if you don't bend
It's not so complicated
If you decide to change your mind
You'll find you're inundated

You're never going to do what you say
You'll always try to make up another way
You're never going to act on your own
You're never going to see that you're all alone

You can't have what you wanted
So make up your mind and come to your senses

You'll never win if you don't bend
It's not so complicated
If you decide to change your mind
You'll find you're inundated

And so you're here and you don't know
if you can choose the way to go
It's not about the way it is
So don't become a realist
You've got time to make a choice
Don't think aloud but have a voice
And when you think the time is right
Don't ever be afraid to fight

You'll never win if you don't bend
It's not so complicated
If you decide to change your mind
You'll find you're inundated

You're never going to see what you like
You're never going to wake up and change your mind

THE COMPROMISE

You fought your way to an inch of freedom
You looked around but it wasn't there
You can't ignore the voice of reason
You can't be what you want,
so you better be what you are

You fought your way to an inch of freedom
You did your best and they didn't care
You've had your share and you have your reasons
You can't be what you want,
so you better be what you are

So we begin our story beleaguered and taken down
Everybody wants a piece of what's going on
Afraid you'll become dull and boring
in a suit that doesn't fit?
Everybody wants a piece of what's going on

You can't mean what you said
You're not sorry for a word of it
Everybody wants to get ahead
Now it's not too late to say you're sorry

You're alright
The Compromise

You've backed yourself into a corner
You looked around and it wasn't there
You're such a sucker for superstition
You can't be what you are,
so you better be what you want

So we begin our story beleaguered and taken down
Everybody wants a piece of what's going on
Afraid you'll become dull and boring
in a suit that doesn't fit?
Everybody wants a piece of what's going on

You can't mean what you said
You're not sorry for a word of it
Everybody wants to get ahead
Now it's not too late to say you're sorry

You're alright
The Compromise

CROSS YOUR HEART AND HOPE TO DIE

I won't be long
I just remembered something
You should go on
before the light behind you fades

Such a shame about the weather
It feels
like it's never going to change

Unbreakable
what's already broken
And so it goes not a word is spoken
And the knife gets twisted deeper with a grin
And it doesn't feel like anything
begin
to slowly fade

Such a shame about the weather
It feels
like it's never going to change

So all along you wanted something
Cross your heart and hope to die
And all along I didn't care
Stick a needle in your eye
I don't blame you for never being there
All together now we crumble
into this

So all along you wanted something
Cross your heart and hope to die
And all along I didn't care
Stick a needle in your eye
I don't blame you for never being there
All together now we crumble
into this

DEAD TO RIGHTS

Leave before you're asked to go
Now that's some good advice!
Don't be sorry you've been warned
We've got you dead to rights

It started getting annoying
Expecting us to kiss the ring
You're never gonna settle for second best
But reality has given you something less

You tried to make us feel like we're not your kind
So now you're back and making up for lost time
Everybody wants redemption
Everybody wants a second chance

Leave before you're asked to go
Now that's some good advice!
Don't be sorry you've been warned
We've got you dead to rights

It's getting very hard to believe
Expecting us to treat you like a king
We're all trying to make our own way
An honest day's work for honest pay

You've worn out your welcome it's such a shame
And now there's nobody but yourself to blame
No one's falling it for it this time
Nobody's going to say that it's alright

Leave before you're asked to go
Now that's some good advice!
Don't be sorry you've been warned
We've got you dead to rights

DEBT

I don’t owe you anything
I don’t owe you anything
I don’t owe you anything
I don’t owe you anything

What now?
Not again
You’re a person
I will never comprehend

I’ve listened
I’ve tried
I can’t change enough
To make you change your mind

I don’t owe you anything
I don’t owe you anything
I don’t owe you anything
I don’t owe you anything

THE DEVIL YOU KNOW (GOD IS A MAN)

It's alright
Everything is fine
You live the perfect life
Never one immoral thought inside your mind

What they say
does it make you feel ashamed?
Isn't everyone the same?
Doesn't matter that it wasn't your idea

God is a man
You know for certain
Thc knowledge in and of itself
is more than we deserve

So you've tried
and you've made up your mind
But something's still not right
The devil you don't know is still outside

What they say
does it make you feel ashamed?
Isn't everyone the same?
Doesn't matter that it wasn't your idea

God is a man
You know for certain
The knowledge in and of itself
is more than we deserve

This song is probably one of the most misunderstood lyrics in the catalog. I remember rehearsing it before there were lyrics written and really loving the music. This was definitely new territory for *face to face*. "The Devil You Know (God is a Man)" was one of the earliest songs written for our controversial album, *Ignorance is Bliss*. We set out to write and record songs that were the most inspiring and compelling to us at the moment. Songs that were influenced by our roots and our current musical tastes, which wasn't a whole lot of punk rock at the time. We followed our intuitions and wrote a more "rock" style record and it was not immediately accepted by our audience, but we were willing to take the risk. Now *Ignorance is Bliss* is one of the most popular records in our catalog.

The music was a departure and I felt like I should equally challenge myself when it came to writing the lyrics. I first wrote the title "The Devil You Know" which is half of the phrase for the old saying, "the devil you know is better than the devil you don't know" and the concept was pretty simple, it was a recognition of the fact that as humans our experiences are both unique and shared and we don't know anything else. This leads to the challenge of established belief systems and the suggestion that what we know may be enough because what we don't know may be worse. Its a question. What if the human experience is as close as we'll ever come to knowing God? It's not necessarily an atheist anthem, but it does question ideas about nearly every established religion and the notion that mankind can never live up to the perfect standard that has been set by them. It's has also been misunderstood because some people have thought that the lyrics make the assertion that God is a "man" as opposed to a woman, which couldn't be any further from my intention. "Man" is used to illustrate 'human' here, not gender.

DISAPPOINTED

Reality is what you want to see
it shouldn't make a difference to me
I put my trust in what you had to say
It didn't make a difference anyway

I know you've tried your very best
and I'm so glad
Thank you so much

Disappointment is what you've made this
Expectations overrated
Disappointment is what you've made this
My ambition is so deflated

Reality is different for me
My eyes are opened wide enough to see
I've listened to your explanations why
The more you fail
the harder that I try

I know you've tried your very best and I'm so glad
Thank you so much

Disappointment is what you've made this
Expectations overrated
Disappointment is what you've made this
My ambition is so deflated

A case of mistaken opportunity
I guess i really got it wrong
Identity is insignificant
or is it everything?

Disappointment is what you've made this
Expectations overrated
Disappointment is what you've made this
My ambition is so deflated

DISCONNECTED

You don't know a thing about me
Is there something that you should know?
I can tell you what you want to hear
Let your inhibitions just go

No, you don't know what you will give up
No, you don't know what you will give up

You don't know what you want
It may take you years to find out
You don't know what you need
It's something that may never come to you

Trust is something that comes easy
When you've never been a victim
Lies and promises and words are said
It's your decision to accept them

No, you don't know what you will give up
No, you don't know what you will give up

You don't know what you want
It may take you years to find out
You don't know what you need
It's something that may never come to you

DISSENSION

and you might think it's possible
for me to think the same way that you do
I've figured out
there's nothing I can do to change my life
and nothing ever will

and you might think it's reasonable
for me to just accept the way it is
I've heard it said
there's nothing I can do to change this world
I wish it wasn't true

There are those who say
The world is ending every day
But I want the chance
I've been waiting here
I try to hide this pain and fear
So give me the chance

and I believe it's rational
to never want to see things the way they are
I've heard it said that
we all carry something to believe
and some can let it go

There are those who say
The world is ending every day
But I want the chance
I've been waiting here
I try to hide this pain and fear
So give me the chance

DO YOU CARE?

Do you want to make a difference?
Do you wonder what would happen if you don't?
Do you need just a little push?
Do you try to change?

Do you think about the other guy?
Do you want just one good reason why you should?
Do you only think about yourself?
Do you want to be left alone?

You're running out of time
and I don't see a change in you
and I don't think you're gonna make it
You're running out of time
and I don't see a change in you
and I don't think you're gonna make it

Do you understand the way it works?
Do you want to take as much as you can get?
Do you need a little push?
Do you try to change?

We're running out of time
and there aren't many changes made
and I don't think we're going to make it
We're running out of time
and there aren't many changes made
and I don't think we're going to make it

DON'T TAKE THE HIGH ROAD

Name your poison
Have your say
Then you best be on your way
I know your kind
You got nothing to lose
Tried to take walk
in a dead man's shoes

Well don't take the high road
It's the road less traveled these days
Stay on the low road
You'll be in good company

Don't take the high road
It's a much more difficult way
Stay on the low road
You'll be in good company
And it leads you right out of that door

Build a fire and watch it burn
There are things you will never learn
Aren't you tired of the same mistakes?
You wonder if you'll ever catch a break

Well don't take the high road
It's the road less traveled these days
Stay on the low road
You'll be in good company

Don't take the high road
It's a much more difficult way
Stay on the low road
You'll be in good company
And it leads you right out of that door

DON'T TURN AWAY

God knows I've tried I've waited in spite of myself
There's nothing to hide
I need you like no one else

I'm sick of trying to figure out where I went wrong
I can't believe these words you say

Don't you turn away from me
I can't say another word I haven't said before
Don't you turn away from me
Don't ask for my apologies I haven't anymore

God knows I'm tired
of lies and denials from you It's down to the wire
I've given myself and that's all I can do

I'm sick of trying to figure out where I went wrong
I can't believe these words you say

Don't you turn away from me
I can't say another word I haven't said before Don't you
turn away from me
Don't ask for my apologies, I haven't anymore

You see that I'm trying
but you turned and walked away
Don't turn away

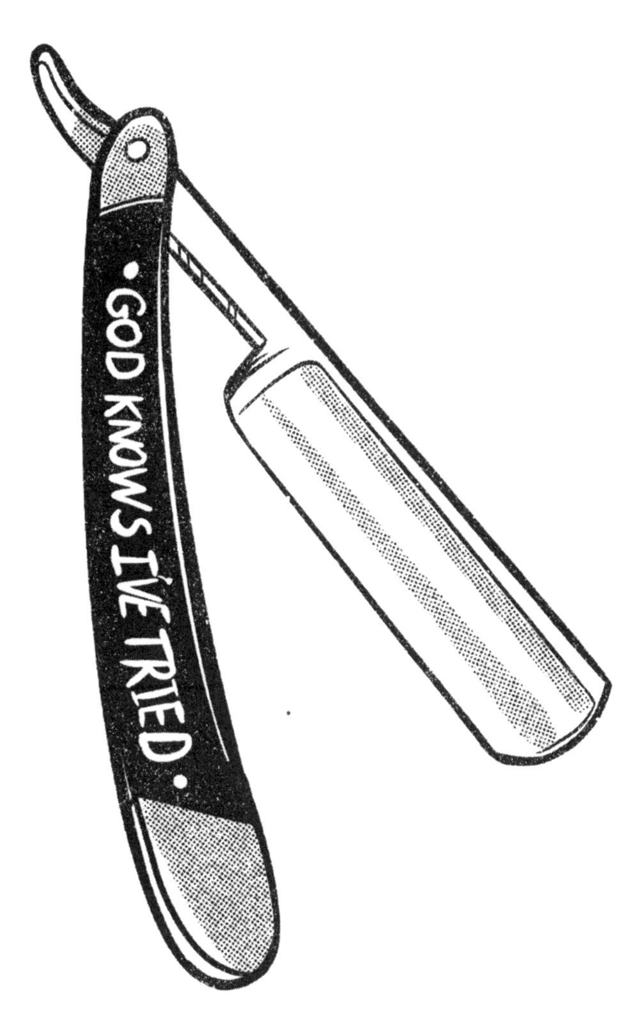
GOD KNOWS I'VE TRIED

DOUBLE CROSSED

Remember when we used to have it made?
It never seemed like we were on the take
but we were double-crossed along the way
It's hard to see it any other way

You're tilted and you're not quite true
I should've done away with you
Telling me the things you knew I wanted
but you were leaving out the best part and
saving it for last

Saving it for last!

Remember when we used to have it made?
It never seemed like we were on the take
but we were double-crossed along the way
It's hard to see it any other way

Jilted and when I came to
I knew I couldn't count on you
Telling me the things I thought I wanted
were just beyond my reach but not my grasp
and I put out my hand

I put out my hand!

Remember when we used to have it made?
It never seemed like we were on the take
but we were double-crossed along the way
It's hard to see it any other way

DOUBLE STANDARD

So what if I'm just a little apprehensive?
So what if I'm not exactly what I've led you to believe?
It doesn't mean a thing

It's a total lie that we're expected to believe
There's no such thing as a level playing field
And I've never been one much for dependency
It's a fraud
your view of equality

So what if you don't believe the double standard?
So what about everybody who comes after are they the same?
Do they deserve a thing?

It's a total lie that we're expected to believe
There's no such thing as a level playing field
And I've never been one much for dependency
It's a fraud
your view of equality

It doesn't matter how hard I have tried
Still I've given everything away with nothing in return
I waited as I watched the world go by
And I've given everything away with no return

It's a total lie that we're expected to believe
There's no such thing as a level playing field
And I've never been one much for dependency
It's a fraud
your view of equality

ESTRANGED

Day after day
You go on living while I wait
It still feels the same
I'm stuck for answers
while you place the blame

I guess it comes to this again
so what's there left to say?
You thought you'd feel no different
now that everything has changed?

I guess it comes to this again
What difference does it make
that you and I think better
of the choices that we've made?

Estranged

It's fading away
I don't remember everything
The words we used to say
seem insignificant today

I guess it comes to this again
so what's there left to say?
You thought you'd feel no different
now that everything has changed?

I guess it comes to this again
What difference does it make
that you and I think better
of the choices that we've made?

EVERYONE HATES A KNOW-IT-ALL

In a flash I'll change the universe
or at least the world I knew
I'm so sick and tired of watching those
who say and never do

And you're right
You're right
You're right

And this waiting seems to last for hours
as I wait impatiently
And it's hard to find the strength inside
to be who I should be

And you're right
You're right
You're right

Why should I believe the words you're telling me are true?
It doesn't seem like anybody feels the way I do
I'm not too proud to say when I was wrong
Everyone hates a know-it-all

So I thought I'd change the universe
and the world I thought i knew
But it seems that change is relative
to what we believe is true

And you're right
You're right
You're right

EVERYTHING IS EVERYTHING

We've got a lot of questions
We've got a lot to learn
So tired of solving problems
Too many bridges burned
We see it all so clearly
and still we close our eyes
why should we understand it?
what good is knowing why?

I know that life can be filled with these changes
I know there's times when it feels like I'm failing but I
I know something in my life will change again

Now I've got a lot of questions
I've got a lot to learn
I'm tired of solving problems
too many bridges burned
I can't change what's in the past
I want to move ahead
I want to understand it
give me the reason why

I know that life can be filled with these changes
I know there's times when it feels like I'm failing but I
I know something in my life will change again

I'm tired of running these circles in my life
I've seen the future it changes before my eyes
and I know that there is something
that's going to change in my life

I know something in my life will change again

EVERYTHING'S YOUR FAULT

Have you heard
them talk about it?
You say they're wrong
but they know all about it
Have you tried another story?
We're tired of all the lies and allegories

Every single thing's your fault
Every single thing's your fault
Every single thing's your fault
Every single thing's your fault

There you are
not really jaded
You've learned to live with being underrated
But they don't know
just what you're made of
Because of them who knows how you will end up?

Every single thing's your fault
Every single thing's your fault
Every single thing's your fault
Every single thing's your fault

With you it's always something
When everyone's the same
don't you try to blame me

Every single thing's your fault
Every single thing's your fault
Every single thing's your fault
Every single thing's your fault

FALLING

It's really easy if you try
To tell another hundred lies
But I'm not going down this time

Just when I think I'm over it
It's getting easy to forget
I haven't even faced it yet

I never wanted anyone to be so wrong for you
Stop falling down

I don't have anyone to blame
I can't make anybody change
I guess there's nothing more to say

I never wanted anyone to be so wrong for you
Stop falling down

I won't believe it if you say that you will change
I won't release you from responsibility
I never wanted to come down on you this way

It's really easy if you try
To tell another hundred lies
But I'm not going down this time

I never wanted anyone to be so wrong for you
Stop falling down

FAREWELL SONG

Lost
I really hate to say I'm lost
but I'm no better off
and now it seems the lines are crossed
feels like I'm going under

But all I ever did was try
that's what I told myself
I knew it was a lie

You called me out back then
You called me out again
I'm out of clever lines

I guess this is goodbye

Wrong
I really hate to say I'm wrong
but you knew better
and you knew it all along
please don't let me go under

But all I ever did was try
that's what I told myself
I knew it was a lie

You called me out back then
You called me out again
I'm out of clever lines

I guess this is goodbye

So were these wasted days and nights?
we were young and we were having the time of our lives

You called me out back then
You called me out again
I'm out of clever lines

But all I ever did was try
that's what I told myself
I knew it was a lie

I guess this is goodbye

FIGHT OR FLIGHT

We're ready to go
ticking like a bomb that's about to blow
It's taking control
pulling at your feet like an undertow

You don't really know
if you're all that capable
But you've been told to

Figure it out!
Don't pretend you're stupid
Sort it out!
Go make yourself useful

You're better than dead
You really made a mess with the words you said
So easily fed
The flames of the fire rise above your head

They want to be led
You've joined the ranks instead
The voice in your head says

Figure it out!
Don't pretend you're stupid
Sort it out!
Go make yourself useful

I can’t figure it out
Any more than the generation before me
I can’t figure it out
How we got where we are today
I can’t figure it out
Any more than the generation before me
I can’t figure it out

We’ve got to fight not to fade away

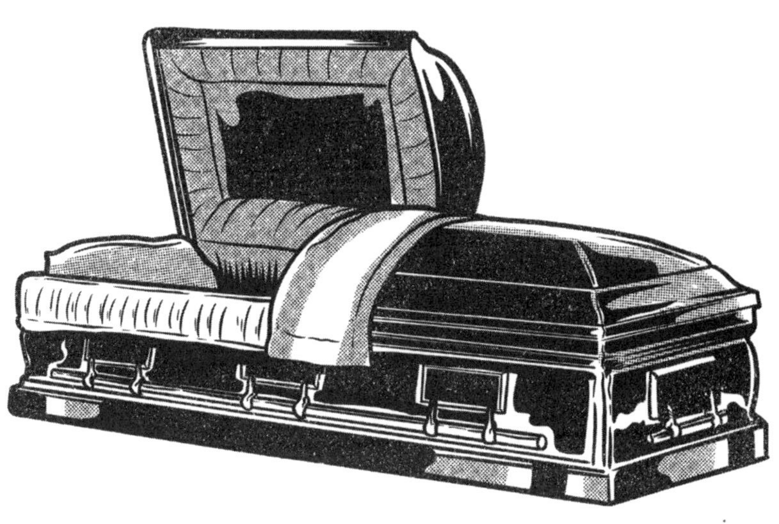

FIGURE IT OUT

So much for the revolution
See what can happen when you make some noise?
So much for your resolution
See what can happen when you make that choice?

And you think you've got it all figured out
And you think you've got it all figured out
And you think you've got it all figured out
And you think you've got it all figured out

Make way for the reputation
You come in like you've never been here before
It's something less than sophistication
The way you come on like a filthy whore

And you think you've got it all figured out
And you think you've got it all figured out
And you think you've got it all figured out
And you think you've got it all figured out

Everybody wants some competition
Everybody wants some compromise
You've been acting of your own volition
Now you're here because you've crossed that line

And you think you've got it all figured out
And you think you've got it all figured out
And you think you've got it all figured out
And you think you've got it all figured out

FIRST STEP, MISSTEP

My life is in a rut and I'm going nowhere
Same sad story, another day
Is there anything else that you want to say?
The words are jumbled up inside your

head is like a piece of clay
molded and shaped by the things they say
First step misstep
stumble then you fall

My eyes are covered up but my faith is stronger
Buying the lie day by day
Try and say the things that you want to say
The words are jumbled up inside your

head is like a piece of clay
molded and shaped by the things they say
First step misstep
stumble then you fall

My pride is beaten up and I'm gonna push back
Down with struggle, take the day
Louder this time listen to what we say
The words are jumbled up inside your

head is like a piece of clay
molded and shaped by the things they say
First step misstep
stumble then you fall

My time is almost up and I'm getting older
Little by little, days are gray
Bothered by the things that you hear them say
The words are jumbled up inside your

head is like a piece of clay
molded and shaped by the things they say
First step misstep
stumble then you fall

FLAT BLACK

He likes it best when there's no choice
He's got option anxiety
He prefers the simple things
until there's something better out there

He has a view but has no voice
The way that it's supposed to be
He's not afraid of anything
except whatever's looming out there

And why should he ever need to change?
He's got nowhere left to go

He loves the radio
It takes him out of his colorless
dull white and flat black

There's a place he's dreaming of
he can't imagine himself there
There will be a risk to take
He makes a calculated effort

It never comes to push and shove
only retreat and disapproving glare
There's never been a choice to make
He knows he'd crack under the pressure

And why should he ever need to change?
He's got nowhere left to go

He loves the radio
It takes him out of his colorless
dull white and flat black

"Flat Black" is from our eighth album *Three Chords and Half Truth*. This record was a nod to all of our favorite British punk rock records and we wore these influences on our sleeves. What was different about this record in particular was the lion's share of the songwriting from the musical standpoint was by Scott. Typically Scott and I will write our own batches of music and then get together and collaborate, but this time Scott was very prolific and I was having some writer's block. I had about twenty or so recordings of song ideas that Scott had given to me and from these I starting writing melodies and lyrics. Again, because this record was a bit of departure from *face to face* (but not a punk rock departure) this time, I wanted to challenge myself as a lyricist to try new things. In particular I wanted to write lyrics that I thought fit with the influences of British punk rock

On this record I tried something different where I wrote all of the song titles first. This was different for me because previously I might start some lyrics with just a line or two that sparked the inspiration for the song. This time I collected a set of titles and gave them themes, then developed the lyrics from that point. "Flat Black" had a cool ring to it and I decided the theme would be how flat black is less flamboyant than say a gloss black and I started to think of the theme of how a person can dull (or flat) when compared to others so I came up with a narrative that was a criticism of people who are dull and boring and focused it on one person for the song. This to me was influenced by one of my favorite British bands Blur. "Flat Black" is a song about becoming too comfortable with your bland routines and comforts. In particular how boring it is to listen to the radio and the garbage they feed you. But it should inspire the reader to not become this cliché but instead to keep life interesting and challenging.

FOR YOU

I have given everything
I have questioned my own faith
Disbelief and discontent
I still remember why I wanted this
for you

When you stumble
When when you fall
They talk about it all
when you fall apart
Is it right for me to wait
when it might be too late?
and still I play the the part

I've pretended I'm alright
I have told a thousand lies
I've become what I despise
I have changed a dozen times
for you

When you stumble
When when you fall
They talk about it all
when you fall apart
Is it right for me to wait
when it might be too late?
and still I play the the part

I've searched for something I can't find
accept the truth with peace of mind

When you stumble
When when you fall
They talk about it all
when you fall apart
Is it right for me to wait
when it might be too late?
and still I play the the part

I have given everything
I have questioned my own faith

FOURTEEN FIFTY-NINE (A HATE SONG)

You look like such a mess
You better shut your gaping mouth
A little bit less than ordinary
We're full of loathing and self-doubt

I'd like to get behind you once
to get a glimpse of that intoxicating light
And shove you all the way in it
I bet you'd hardly fight

Fourteen fifty-nine
It shouldn't be too long before you die
Fourteen fifty-nine
I hope it won't be long until you die

This is a hate song
Will you please shut your gaping mouth?
But don't leave us out of the conversation
Yeah I know what you're all about

I'd like to get behind you once
To get a glimpse of that intoxicating light
And shove you all the way in it
I bet you'd hardly fight

Fourteen fifty-nine
It shouldn't be too long before you die
Fourteen fifty-nine
I hope it won't be long until you die

Fourteen fifty-nine
It shouldn't be too long before you die
Fourteen fifty-nine
I hope it won't be long until you die

FUNDAMENTALIST

Honor, duty , loyalty, and vigilance
God and country
wisdom and benevolence

It feels good to you, doesn't it?
Like a lovely fairytale
It's what they taught you wasn't it?
And in the cross you bear another nail

Fundamentalist
Prove to them that your God exists
Fundamentalist
The greater the cost the more they resist

Anger, hated, irresponsibility
Violence, vengeance
take the opportunity

This feels right to you, doesn't it?
Like you ever had a choice
It's making sense to you isn't it?
Just concentrate and listen to that voice

Fundamentalist
Prove to them that your God exists
Fundamentalist
The greater the cost the more they resist

Disinformation
Fascination
Indoctrination
Lies
Guilty by association
Suffocation
you would take a life
to demonstrate your reverence for all things living?
...right

Aspirations
Complications
Suffering and pain
Inspiration
Trepidation
Vindication
Make them pay!
Because you believe in what is right
and that makes it okay?

Fundamentalist
Prove to them that your God exists
Fundamentalist
The greater the cost the more they resist

Fundamentalist
Prove to them that your God exists
Fundamentalist
The greater the cost the more they resist

GET UP

Come on get up
and pull yourself together
or sure enough
you'll be right back here tomorrow
I know it's tough
You walk a mile in these shoes
you've had enough
We go right back where we started

The walls are crumbling down
Are you ready to make a go?
Another demon right outside your door
Are you ready to let it go?
Didn't we have this conversation before?
We must have had this conversation once before?

It's not because of you
It's nothing more than merely
just a lack of concentration

Come on get up
and give us what we want
or sure enough
we'll have nothing left to show for it
You're so fed up
of jumping through these hoops
for everyone
We go right back where we started

The walls are crumbling down
Are you ready to make a go?
Another demon right outside your door
Are you ready to let it go?
Didn't we have this conversation before?
We must have had this conversation once before?

It's not because of you
It's nothing more than merely
just a lack of concentration

GRADED ON A CURVE

It's a waste of time
It's a race that can't be won
Call the whole thing off
Well that's easier said than done

And I try to shut it out
And I think I've figured out
That it makes no sense
to compare what I've done

So what do I do now that I'm alone?
I've been building up and tearing down
and looking for what never can be found

So what do I do now that I'm alone?
God I tried so hard to get here
but still I'm averaged out
Graded on a curve

Put the blinders on
and believe in someone else
You're not what they want
that's exactly what they sell
And it's all been preordained
but it's never quite the same
Once you've figured out
that it makes no sense

So what do I do now that I'm alone?
I've been building up and tearing down
and looking for what never can be found

So what do I do now that I'm alone?
God I tried so hard to get here
but still I'm averaged out
Graded on a curve

And I don't care
if I'm the one who makes mistakes
And I don't care how long this is going to take
Does it really matter how you played the game
when you were never really in it?

It's a waste of time
Call the whole thing off
Half Asleep

Wake up now this time
You've been hiding
underneath the covers of your bed again
It's alright
I thought that I
could make this into anything I wanted
Suppose that I've forgotten how to dream?

We could steal a little time away
and think of something more to say
to make it seem like it's alright
I thought that I
might feel something different this time
instead I don't feel anything at all

Are you a wake
or am I talking to myself?
Because I was hoping you weren't listening
You're such a fake
and I don't know if I can tell
I wish that I could fall asleep again

Wake up now this time
You're not fooling anyone
pretending that you're still asleep
But I don't mind
You said if I
woke up then I might never be able
to get myself to fall asleep again

Are you a wake
or am I talking to myself?
Because I was hoping you weren't listening
You're such a fake
and I don't know if I can tell
I wish that I could fall asleep again

HANDOUT

What's it going to take to be done?
What's it going to be right or wrong?
I don't have the strength left to fight
I don't have to make up my mind

I know you're never wrong no matter what it takes
I know you're not the one but we all make mistakes
Help me out

What's it going to take to be done?
What's it going to be right or wrong?
I don't have the strength left to fight
I don't have to make up my mind

I know you're never wrong no matter what it takes
I know you're not the one but we all make mistakes
Help me out

I don't want your handout
I don't need your way out

So what's it going to be?
I've done everything
Why won't you believe
you're the same as me?

What's it going to take to be done?
What's it going to be right or wrong?
I don't have the strength left to fight
I don't have to make up my mind

I don't want your handout
I don't need your way out

HARD CASE

There's no way he's gonna get there
but that's never stopped him before
Someday he's gonna show them
Dusts himself off and gets up off the floor

Pulls himself together
Stands up tall and grins
Straightens out his clothes
He's ready for another round again

You're looking at a hard case

They came around and asked about him
But he slipped out the back door
Nobody knows, nobody's talking
But you can be sure that he knows the score

Pulls himself together
Stands up tall and grins
Straightens out his clothes
He's ready for another round again

You're looking at a hard case

A nobody just some so-and-so
A face you might think you used to know
so bring it down and swing it low
He doesn't lose
because doesn't know how to quit

Looking at a hard case
Staring at a plain face
Looking at a hard case
Staring at a plain face

HEART OF HEARTS

Close your eyes and try to get to sleep now
Don't you make a peep now
We hear everything

Shut the door and make it clean and neat now
You've been so discreet now
We've seen everything
Inside your heart of hearts you know

Pick yourself up off the floor and stand now
You're acting like a man now
You've got everything

Forget about the places that you've been now
Wash away your sin now
You've got everything
Inside your heart of hearts you know
Will you choose to hide it in your soul?

If it's wrong and I'm feeling so indifferent
I might be in danger of myself

Shut your mouth and get yourself to sleep now
Don't let them hear you weep now
You've got everything
Inside your heart of hearts you know
Will you choose to hide it in your soul?

If it's wrong and I'm feeling so indifferent
I might be in danger of myself

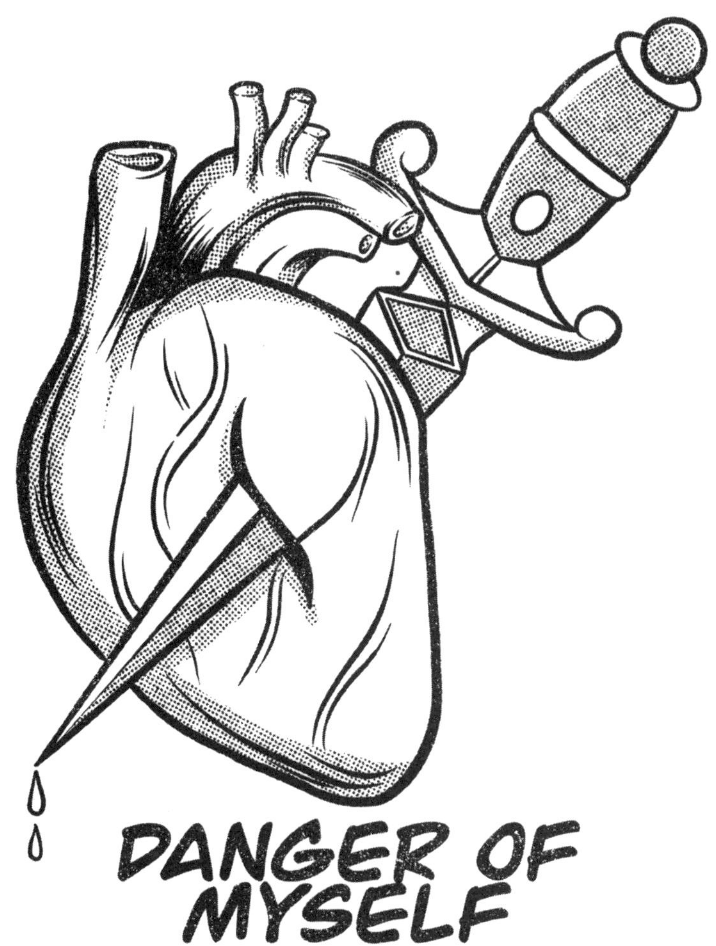

DANGER OF MYSELF

HOLLOW

I'll never feel again
I'll never feel again
Then I won't have to feel this pain I'm in

If it sounds familiar
because nothing ever goes the way I planned
If it sounds peculiar
then you don't have to try and understand

I'll never feel again
I'll never feel again
Then I won't have to feel this pain I'm in

I'm not a great example
of everything the world expects of us
I know I'm no exception
I've questioned everything I used to trust
A question of necessity or lust

I'll never feel again
I'll never feel again
Then I won't have to feel this pain I'm in

It's as simple as you make it
and as complicated
as who you think you are

NEVER
FEEL
AGAIN!!

HOW TO RUIN EVERYTHING

There's something wrong with me I don't know
if it's not just inside my head
It feels like I'm walking through a dream
I still remember what you said

I know that everything will be alright
It's going to work out for the best
I think there must be something better still
It isn't really so far-fetched

You know I'll go running out and ruin everything

It's hard to trust in somebody else
responsible for your success
But in the end I know it's up to me
I live my life with no regrets
So tell me everything I want to hear
What do you like about me best?
I've been a king and I've been a fool
I'm not about to give up yet

You know I'll go running out and ruin everything

I DON'T MIND AND YOU DON'T MATTER

Enough
How much is enough?
I'm tired of keeping up
I'm tired of treading water all the time

I'm done
but I won't be the one
who tries to get ahead
by standing on the backs of other men

It may sound simple-minded I don't care
It's never really
been about what they think anyway

I'm still here and I'm okay
doesn't matter anyway
I guess I should be sorry, I'm not
You would be the last thing on my mind

I'm fine
and I don't really mind
I barely have the time
but I'll admit I don't care anyway

I know
it's probably getting old
to hear the reasons why
the world is ending every other day

It may sound simple-minded I don't care
It's never really
been about what they think anyway

I'm still here and I'm okay
doesn't matter anyway
I guess I should be sorry, I'm not
You would be the last thing on my mind

But I get closer all the time
I've come full circle
and I'm almost where I started from
In spite of all that I have done
Never going back
Never going back
Gonna turn myself around and
I'm still here and I'm okay
doesn't matter anyway
I guess I should be sorry, I'm not
You would be the last thing on my mind

I'm still here and I'm okay
doesn't matter anyway
I guess I should be sorry, I'm not
You would be the last thing on my mind

I KNOW WHAT YOU ARE

Even if it makes you want to stop and stare
You'd be better off it you were unaware
Everybody wants to see that it's not them

Focused and unaffected
You'll get what you expected

You're boring and predictable
Doesn't everybody want to get their hands
on everything that they desire?

I know you're not afraid
and I know exactly what you want to be

Even still you want to take what you can't get
You'd be better off if you could just forget
There isn't anyone who lives without regret

Focused and unaffected
You'll get what you expected

You're boring and predictable
Doesn't everybody want to get their hands
on everything that they desire?

I know you're not afraid
and I know exactly what you want to be

So it seems to be that no one really cares
And so the struggle to achieve the lion's share
and I know what you are
I know what you are
I know what you are
I know what you are
I'm not what you are

I KNOW YOU WELL

Try not to try
Try not to care
It's really easy once you learn that no one is listening

Try not to give
Try not to help
You'll do much better for yourself
because nothing else matters

I know you well by now
You're that "good" person

Don't be afraid
Don't be naive
You think you're better than me
well you're sadly mistaken

I know you well by now
You're that "good" person

It's all the same inside our minds
Everything is justified
What is wrong and what is right
Everything is justified

Try not to try
Try not to care
It's really easy once you learn that no one is listening

Try not to give
Try not to help
You'll do much better for yourself bec
ause nothing else matters

I know you well by now
You're that "good" person

I'M NOT AFRAID

I didn't want a second chance
Now that's exactly where I am
Back where I didn't want to be
Back where I knew you'd find me out

I've never been afraid of you
I never will admit the truth
I know there's something I can do

I'm not afraid to face myself
But is it me or something else
that makes me exactly what I am?
That's something I will always doubt

I've never been afraid of you
I never will admit the truth
I know there's something I can do

"I'm Not Afraid" is the the first song I had written that I heard on the radio. It was on a late night radio show that aired on Sunday nights in Los Angeles. I remember we were driving to play a club show and we heard it in the car on the way down. It is one of the first songs I ever wrote for *face to face* during our formative years. There's something about the honesty and simplicity of this song that endured and became a sort of blueprint in forming the sound and lyrical style of *face to face*. The lyrics are defiant but also vulnerable at the same time.

The first line of the second verse, "I'm not afraid to face myself" reveals the theme of the lyrics. It's a song about the internal struggle to become better. The person I'm singing about having no fear of is actually myself, or rather that part of myself who keeps me from becoming better and the declaration of defiance is meant to be a catalyst for positive personal change. I'm not sure if I actually knew any of this when I wrote these lyrics, but as I read over them now, nearly thirty years later, I am convinced that this was what I was trying to say whether I knew it at the time or not.

I have been accused of writing in a somewhat vague way in my early lyric writing and in hindsight, I can't say that I disagree with that notion but I think it's pretty clear what the intent was with these lyrics even if it isn't well defined. It's about overcoming the fear of change, especially personal change and growth to become better. There are moments in the song when you almost hear the internal struggle and rationalization. In the second verse the line, "is it me or something else that makes me exactly what I am?" is an attempt to rationalize fault with environmental and external forces rather than accept your shortcomings, own them, and overcome them.

I'M TRYING

A four-year-old at play
shot and killed today
never even had a chance
Seventeen and high
threw away his life
has a gun to feel like he's a man
Can't have it any other way

Laying in the street asking for a drink
doesn't have a place to live
Pregnant at thirteen
still can hear the screams
something that she never will forget
Can't have it any other way

I'm trying to open my mind
I'm trying to open my mind

So you can keep your faith
because I'll just walk away
There's no reason for me to stay

Can't have it any other way
Can't have it any other way

I'm trying to open my mind
I'm trying to open my mind
I'm trying to open my mind
I'm trying to make up my mind

I, ME, MINE

Do what you're told
Do what they say
and do it all you want as long as it's the right way

Just do your best
Give all you can
The harder that you try
the better chance things go as planned

Seems like you want to sit around and talk about it
but I've got something else in mind
You know there's nothing left for us to talk about so
it's become a waste of time

You'll never know until you've suffered
You'll never know until you've cried
You'll never know until you've bled out for them

Because in the end it's only you and you alone
That's why I'm looking out for I, me, mine

You're bought and sold
That's what they say
and is this what you wanted bills you can't afford to pay?
They're not impressed
You had your chance
You're like a puppet with a broken string
who won't dance

Seems like you want to sit around and talk about it
but I've got something else in mind
You know there's nothing left for us to talk about so
it's become a waste of time

You'll never know until you've suffered
You'll never know until you've cried
You'll never know until you've bled out for them

Because in the end it's only you and you alone
That's why I'm looking out for I, me, mine

I USED TO THINK

I've tried to fake it
I've tried to lie about it
I've tried to take it
There's nothing new about it

I can't take a thing from you
because I want what I want
and it wouldn't do
I've tried to make it
There's nothing you can say

I used to think that things were going to be okay
I never wanted to think
there would be another way
Is there another way?

I've tried to fake it
I've tried to lie about it
I've tried to make it
I didn't realize it

I can't take a thing from you
because I want what I want
and it wouldn't do
I've tried to make it
There's nothing you can say

I used to think that things were going to be okay
I never wanted to think
there would be another way
Is there another way?

I WANT

Everybody wants the truth
but everybody lies
yeah everybody lies
Everybody wants some proof
but everybody's blind
so open up your eyes

I really don't know much of
anything at all
but I'll admit we're all the same
You ask forgiveness and you
make the same mistakes
And I'll admit we're all the same

So I say
I want to know
do these words mean anything?
How can my life
mean something more than what it seems?

Everybody wants equality
but we're all prejudiced
yeah we're all hypocrites
Everybody wants the world
but we have nothing

I really don’t know much of
anything at all
but I’ll admit we’re all the same
You ask forgiveness and you
make the same mistakes
And I’ll admit we’re all the same

So I say
I want to know
do these words mean anything?
How can my life
mean something more than what it seems?

I WON'T LIE DOWN

Does anybody see him?
another set up for the fall
Does anybody hear him?
He's screaming at the same blank wall

Everyone can't be right
but everyone will decide

I'm not afraid of the price I pay
I won't lie down as you walk away
I'm not afraid of the price I pay
I won't lie down as you walk away

I'm sure you must have seen him
I know you must have heard it all
I know you used to be him
did anybody care at all?

Everyone can't be right
but everyone will decide

I'm not afraid of the price I pay
I won't lie down as you walk away
I'm not afraid of the price I pay
I won't lie down as you walk away

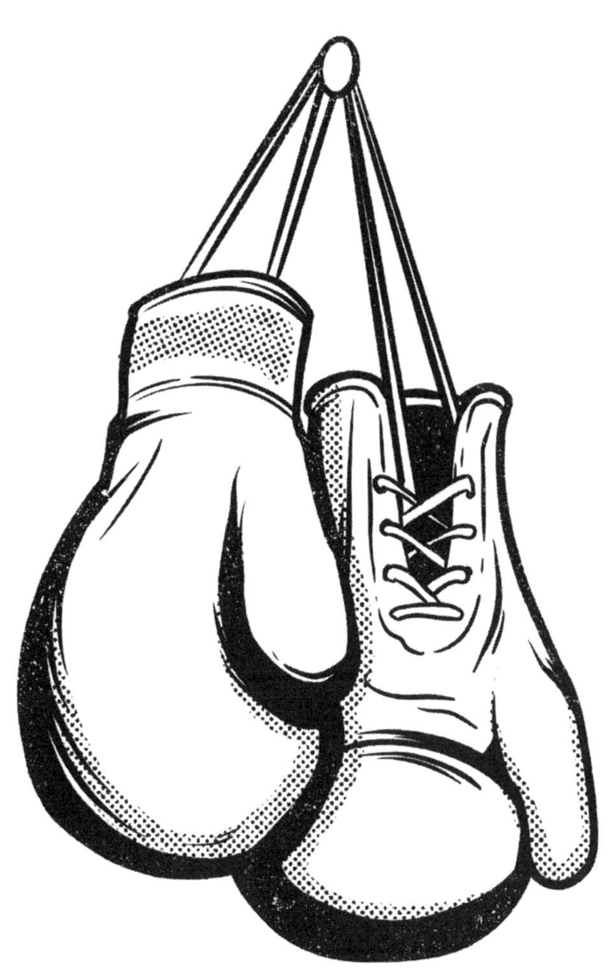

I WON'T SAY I'M SORRY

Make up your mind
Are you really becoming this?
Are you going along to get along?
I hope I got it wrong

You know I've tried
and it's hard for me to resist
There's a point to be made
and a line to cross
no matter what it costs

Am I supposed to be afraid?
Should I be careful what I say?
You never listened anyway
It doesn't make a difference

I won't say I'm sorry
I won't take back a single word
This is exactly how I feel
I won't say I'm sorry
Take me exactly at my word
It doesn't matter how you feel

You're out of line
but instead I'm the one to blame
And I'm sickened by how we buy the lie
and no one seems to mind

Am I supposed to be afraid?
Should I be careful what I say?
You never listened anyway
It doesn't make a difference

I won't say I'm sorry
I won't take back a single word
This is exactly how I feel
I won't say I'm sorry
Take me exactly at my word
It doesn't matter how you feel

I can't see things the way you meant for them to be
I must be blind
On this, I think we both agree

"I Won't Say I'm Sorry" is from our record *Protection.* This record represented a kind of homecoming for us as it was our return to the record label that we released our debut album *Don't Turn Away* on; Fat Wreck Chords. In the 1990s, the punk rock community was obsessed with the idea of "selling out." This meant many things and all of them were interpreted by fanzine contributors and other judgmental scenesters who would call a band out for the smallest infraction. The worst offense however, was signing a record deal with a major label which of course we did right after our debut record. I wanted to do what I thought was right for the band regardless of arbitrary rules set by the established punk rock community. This led to criticism but worse yet it led to us jumping from label to label throughout most of our career. The move back to Fat Wreck was a leap forward in stability and I think for the most part, appeased the punk rock gods.

I have written about departures the band has taken on some of the records in our catalog, but this one was a return to our roots. I wanted the lyrics to be representative of this but I didn't want to retread old ideas. I think "I Won't Say I'm Sorry" is the perfect example of this. I think the title aptly conveys the theme, but more specifically the lyrics are about watching a group of people adopting a philosophy of group think and letting it cover their identities to the point of losing their moral character. It is an assertion of one's personal character, philosophy, and morals despite the fact that they may be unpopular or even offensive to certain groups and the right to have an individual viewpoint. It is about conveying one's own convictions and to remain unapologetic for it.

ICONS

I think it's starting again
The same thing that happens when
I'm sure what I'm thinking is right
but I don't know anything

The inhibitions decline
Decided to make up my mind
I'm sure what I'm thinking is right
But I don't know anything

So why are you looking to me for the answers?
It's only the truth if you want to believe in it

Everyone wants to live another life
So many aspirations have been placed upon you

I'm not sure where to begin
I've taken a lot on the chin
and everyone else seems to win
and I don't have anything

So who am I to decide?
I've tried my best and I've tried
to make everything feel alright
but I don't know anything

So why are you looking to me for the answers?
It's only the truth if you want to believe it is

Everyone wants to live another life
So many aspirations have been placed upon you

Convinced that this is what you want
Are you really sure you know it all?

So willing to trust in anyone

Confused by what they call the truth
The only thing you know for sure
is you don't trust a single thing
about yourself

Everyone wants to live another life
So many aspirations have been placed upon you

IN HARM'S WAY

Where did you go?
So far away
It seems like everybody tried to tell you everything
And who are you?
Who are they?
Seems like everybody wants to give themselves away

Three days old anyway
So you're tired
and the inspiration's gone away
Where are you?
In harm's way
Seems like everything is broken

And it feels like I might break on this ordinary day
Why do we need to change?
When we were perfect yesterday?

Having trouble comprehending
I was sure that I was who I thought I was
And if you want the truth
then I blame them, I blame you, and I blame myself

In all this pomp and circumstance
I failed to see that I had missed my chance
Without a word to say I waited
as you turned and walked away

And it feels like I might break on this ordinary day
Why do we need to change?
When we were perfect yesterday?

INCOMMUNICADO

Did you get the message?
Somebody killed the messenger I guess
We may never speak again

But it seems like we're getting closer
seems like we're getting closer
It seems like we're getting over
It seems like we're going under

Thank you for your patience
Please continue holding
Your estimated waiting time is something only
used to discourage you

no answer, no return

Incommunicado
Can't hear what they're saying
Shouldn't someone tell them there's no point in waiting?
We've got to bury this
It's time to move on

Did you get the message?
Somebody killed the messenger I guess
We may never speak again

IT ALMOST ALL WENT WRONG

This uphill battle I've been fighting my whole life
Somehow this melody cuts deeper than their knives
These three chords can win this war
and it's not even a fair fight

Forget about yourself for just a while

I didn't really feel like singing this song
I've finally made it back where you were all along
It almost ended tragically
It almost all went wrong
I didn't really feel like singing this song

If I was afraid to fail I wouldn't even try
I won't be written off, I won't let them decide
For what it's worth this doesn't work
unless you're hanging on these lines

Forget about yourself for just a while

I didn't really feel like singing this song
I've finally made it back where you were all along
It almost ended tragically
It almost all went wrong
I didn't really feel like singing this song

Do you ever feel
like we were meant for something better still?
Well, maybe not
but forget about yourself for just a while

I didn't really feel like singing this song
I've finally made it back where you were all along
It almost ended tragically
It almost all went wrong
I didn't really feel like singing this song

IT'S NOT ALL ABOUT YOU

You start in the middle and you're doing fine
But there's just too little to keep you satisfied
So you try a little harder
and you try and try
It's a long way up so you go for a ride

I said everybody wants to have it made
They don't wanna do nothing
but they still get paid
So you ride a little further and it starts to change
Did you think that everything was gonna be the same?

I said it's not all about you
You're so cynical and vain
And I know you'd rather die than take the blame

It's not all about you
You're so cynical and vain
God I swear you can't get out of your own way

Now you made your way up and you like the view
But it gets a little boring when there's nothing to do
So you look to the middle
but it's nothing new
Everybody wants to be the same as you

I said everything's gonna be the same
And it doesn't matter
if they ever knew your name
So you better take the money and forget the fame
or get back in the middle and get out of the game

I said it's not all about you
You're so cynical and vain
And I know you'd rather die than take the blame

It's not all about you
You're so cynical and vain
God I swear you can't get out of your own way

So it's down to the bottom and there's nothing to say
I think everybody knew that it would be this way
It's the same old story
and it's such a shame
So make yourself at home because we're here to stay
I said it's not all about you
You're so cynical and vain
And I know you'd rather die than take the blame

It's not all about you
You're so cynical and vain
God I swear you can't get out of your own way

IT'S NOT OVER

You think you're over with it
Don't want to talk about it
I'll tell you something you don't want to know

You think you're over with it
Don't want to talk about it
I'll tell you something you don't want to know

So what's the problem with my life?
Don't over complicate it
Let's stop with all this wasting time
I feel you all around
There's nothing else that I can see
Anything is better than nothing

I'll try and try
I won't be denied
I want my chance
I want what's mine

JACKBOOTED THUG

Down before I knew what hit me
stripped of my defenses
The ringing in me ears is deafening
Hands secured behind my back

I can't think or speak my mind
I can't lend an ear to hear

Assume the position
You're part of the system
The execution is brutal
Resistance is futile

Torn my liberty behind me
taken like innocence
The buzzing in my head is threatening
Hands wringing in my lap

I can't think or speak my mind
I can't lend an ear to hear

Assume the position
You're part of the system
the execution is brutal
Resistance is futile

I can't think or speak my mind
I can't lend an ear to hear

Assume the position
You're part of the system
The execution is brutal
Resistance is futile

JINXPROOF

Running from something and making up lies
but desperate to not fade away
Everyone else wants to say what they need to say
We needed to get out from the decay

We're jinxproof

Down like an anchor and sinking too fast
It's such a boring cliche
Everyone's taking down someone else with the weight
We needed to get out from the decay

We're jinxproof

Forget all this talk of bad luck
And those who say we're born to lose
You and I don't need a good luck charm
I know you never meant me any harm

But even if I kept a four leaf clover
You know I'm telling you the truth

We're jinxproof

JUST LIKE YOU SAID

And now that all is said and done
It's kind of hard to hold my tongue
Because you still don't believe you're wrong

I'm not so sure what I would say
If I could talk to you that way
You wouldn't understand

I was foolish from the start
I've tried not to fall apart
It's just like you said but everything is somehow different

I've tried hard not to admit
that there was some truth to it
It's just like you said but everything is somehow different

Have you ever imagined what you think
the way your circumstance would be
and fixed a picture in your head?

I guess you've thought of everything
I'm sure you know much more than me
At least that's what you think

I was foolish from the start
I've tried not to fall apart
It's just like you said but everything is somehow different

I’ve tried hard not to admit
that there was some truth to it
It’s just like you said but everything is somehow different
It shouldn’t have to make you wonder
I thought you knew it all along
How I was innocent and pure
and you were smug and so demure
When you predicted I would fall

I was foolish from the start
I’ve tried not to fall apart
It’s just like you said but everything is somehow different

I’ve tried hard not to admit
that there was some truth to it
It’s just like you said but everything is somehow different

KEEP YOUR CHIN UP

It's a contradiction wrapped up in a cliche
It's the old catch twenty-two
They'll gently nudge you back into the margins
It's do as I say not as I do

You're on the ropes again it's time to make a play
Dig deep and find the strength
There's just no other way

I know it seems like no one's in your corner
I know you've thought of throwing in the towel
It's hard to take it when you're hit below the belt again
but I know you don't want to go back to the beginning

Keep your chin up
when they try and bring you down

Well I've been called a lot worse than a cliche
And I've seen a lot since I was twenty-two
Don't ever let yourself fall in the margins
It doesn't matter what you say but what you do

You're on the ropes again it's time to make a play
Dig deep and find the strength
There's just no other way

I know it seems like no one's in your corner
I know you've thought of throwing in the towel
It's hard to take it when you're hit below the belt again
but I know you don't want to go back to the beginning

Keep your chin up
when they try and bring you down

LATE

I don't know where I belong
all I know is that I'm wrong
I can't wait another day
make it all just go away
I don't want it today

I don't want to be late
If you knew what I knew
you wouldn't be willing to wait
Don't be fooled by what you read it's not the same as
what you see
You're trying to sell me
and it's something for nothing
I don't want to be late

I don't know where I belong
all I know is that I'm wrong
I can't wait another day
make it all just go away
I don't want it today

I don't want to be late
If you knew what I knew
you wouldn't be willing to wait
Don't be fooled by what you read it's not the same as
what you see
You're trying to sell me
and it's something for nothing
I don't want to be late

LONG WAY DOWN

You're not the same as yesterday
You shouldn't listen to what they say
Their path is crooked
and you should know
before you go
that it's a long way down

Carved your own path and made your way
They're on attack, it's so cliche
you step sure-footed
but you should know
before you go
that it's a long way down

So much at stake
not much to wager
The odds were never in your favor
You broke away
despite the danger
It still means everything

They're reveling in your dismay
You're so afraid of what they'll say
now loosely rooted
you should know
before you go
that it's a long way down
So much at stake
not much to wager

The odds were never in your favor
You broke away
despite the danger
It still means everything

LOST

And all I thought I want I lost it all tonight
And all I thought I want I lost it all tonight

Do you know
there's only so much you control?
You can try to save my soul if you like
But I'm sure this time it's no different

And all I thought I want I lost it all tonight
And all I thought I want I lost it all tonight

Do you know
there's only so much you control?
You can try to save my soul if you like
But I'm sure this time it's no different

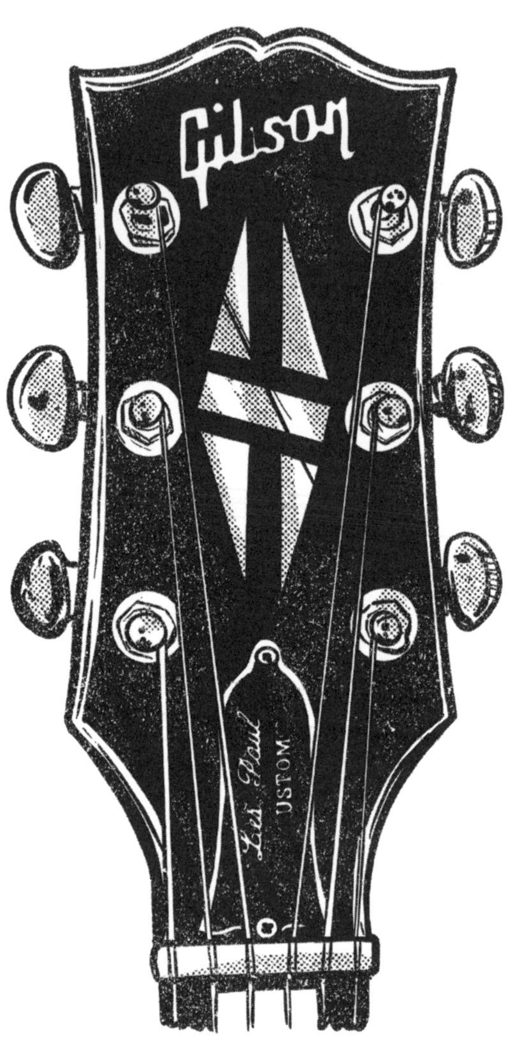
Gibson
Les Paul
USTOM

MANIPULATE - CAPITULATE

You want it so badly
It's the only thing you've ever wanted
Acceptance
Friends
Popularity

They hate you so vehemently
You represent everything they hate about this world
Weakness
Compassion,
Vulnerability

Manipulate
Capitulate

They descend upon you as subtle as a heart attack
Compliments
Praise
Reassurance

You follow like a lamb innocently to the slaughter
Deceit
Lies
Treachery

Manipulate
Capitulate

You hate him the way you hate yourself
He represents everything you hate in this world
Innocence
Joy
Inexperience

It's the only thing he's ever wanted
And you're going to give it to him

Manipulate
Capitulate

MARKED MEN

Friday night, three AM
Sink into that place again
You don't know me anymore

Lay my head down on the rack
It was yesterday I just got back
I don't know if I will never sleep again

It looks like we might have to go
Something's telling me our cover's blown
There's got to be a better way
Running like we're marked men there's no light of day

Inch by inch, killing time
Heading for the county line
A voice inside tells me to wait

No control, fading fast
Not sure how long this can last
And I don't like what I've become

It looks like we might have to go
Something's telling me our cover's blown
There's got to be a better way
Running like we're marked men there's no light of day

Set it up, knock it down
Three days and another town
Someone's following behind

Take a breath, slow it down
Clench my fist and stand my ground
You won't see me anymore

It looks like we might have to go
Something's telling me our cover's blown
There's got to be a better way
Running like we're marked men there's no light of day

MAYBE NEXT TIME

Did you hear that?
It sounds like I'm losing my faith
Did you feel that?
It feels like I'm so far away

But if l knew what I know now
This wouldn't be so wrong
Now I'm back to where I started from

And if I was sure then I'd be right
But I guess I've lost this fight
Wait until the next time

I can feel it
It feels like my luck's going to change
I can see it
It seems like this time it's okay

But if l knew what I know now
This wouldn't be so wrong
Now I'm back to where I started from

And if I was sure then I'd be right
But I guess I've lost this fight
Wait until the next time

I know I was close that time before
There's still a need for something more
Wait until the next time

MELANCHOLICS ANONYMOUS

I will come back to my senses
I will try and start again

It's almost like I never even took a single step
I thought that I was getting somewhere
I hadn't even left
I'll be okay
I will be saved

I will pull myself together
I will come up with a plan

It's almost like I never even took a single step
I thought that I was getting somewhere
I hadn't even left
I'll be okay
I will be saved

Do you know my name?
It's written in my breath on the windowpane

I will remember what I'm made of
I will turn it all around

It's almost like I never even took a single step
It felt like I was getting somewhere
I hadn't even left
But I'll be okay I will be saved

Do you know my name?
It's written in my breath on the windowpane

MERRY CHRISTMAS

Now I feel a lot better but I
still can't find the cheer
I want to tell you about the way I feel
but I can't be sincere
I thought we had this figured out
but I guess it wasn't clear
And I hoped that we'd be better off this year

We started out a little late I guess
It's Christmastime again
And you're not happy about the way it feels
now that we are only friends
I thought I had you figured out
But it's now and that was then
And I hope that we aren't starting up again

Merry Christmas
And I hope you're happy here
Merry Christmas
And I hope that you get everything
that you deserve this year

Now I feel a little older
and I'm not sure how I got here
Doesn't matter what I figured out
It's going to be the same this year
I guess we made a big mistake but it isn't very clear
And I hoped that we'd be better off this year

Merry Christmas
And I hope you're happy here
Merry Christmas
And I hope that you get everything
that you deserve this year

MIDDLING AROUND

I don't know what to tell you
I know it's probably unfair
You've got to be willing to open your eyes
and see for yourself
You probably don't have a prayer

I've been trying to tell you
Not sure if you're aware
Everyone's trying to take all they can
You barely exist
You probably don't have a prayer

I hope you weren't counting on someone
to show you the way

Are you telling me nobody cares at all?
Don't ask me to say that you're wrong
You're probably safe in the middle
right where you belong

I've got something to tell you
There's no need to despair
You've got to be willing to be more than present
And ready to bleed
You probably don't have a prayer

It's not like it's just going to happen someday
I hope you weren't counting on someone
to show you the way

Does it seem like there's nobody there at all?
Edging outside all along
Just get yourself back in the middle
right where you belong

NEARLY IMPOSSIBLE

Please excuse my point of view
and allow me to intrude
I have given up on what I thought I knew
And our ignorance is bliss
So we're hiding out in it
And I guess it doesn't matter what we've missed

Would it scare you away if I was sixty-five feet tall?
Would it make you afraid if there was nothing left at all?
Nothing left at all

Its nearly impossible
Highly improbable
But not hopeless

We are swallowed up in it
And its neither here nor there
So it makes no sense that anyone would care
And it feels like innocence
when you chose to not resist
We fulfill our needs at everyone's expense

Would it scare you away if l was sixty-five feet tall?
Would it make you afraid if there was nothing left at all?
Nothing left at all

Its nearly impossible
Highly improbable
But not hopeless

IT'S NEVER GOING TO BE THE SAME

You listened to that little voice in your head
but you got it all wrong
There wasn't anything you could have said
And now it's been too long

If I can't make you understand
It doesn't have to be this way
I wont give you the upper hand
And now I'm backed into a corner

You've got to open your eyes up
Before you make the same mistakes
You've got to open your eyes up
It may already be too late
It's never going to be the same

You listened to that little voice in your head
but you got it all wrong

If I can't make you understand
It doesn't have to be this way
I wont give you the upper hand
And now I'm backed into a corner

You've got to open your eyes up
Before you make the same mistakes
You've got to open your eyes up
It may already be too late
It's never going to be the same

I can't watch as you fade away
I've never seen you act this way
I know you lost the words to say but hold on

If I can't make you understand
It doesn't have to be this way
I wont give you the upper hand
And now I'm backed into a corner

You've got to open your eyes up
Before you make the same mistakes
You've got to open your eyes up
It may already be too late
It's never going to be the same

THE NEW WAY

You're alright, you're alive, you're the number one
They said that you're not ashamed of what you've done
Everyone makes mistakes
Make it up you'll be okay
That's what they tell you

You won't get the special treatment
I don't care what you do or say
Don't let them tell you what you're already thinking I
t's a no win situation

Well enough of the old way
It's not working and the rules have already changed
What we need is a new way
There's something else just a little bit better
It's on the way

You're a drag, you're a bore, you're a rainy day
You take offense to almost everything they do or say
Everyone makes mistakes
Make it up you'll be okay
I should've told you

You won't get the special treatment
I don't care what you do or say
Don't let them tell you what you're already thinking
It's a no win situation

Well enough of the old way
It's not working and the rules have already changed
What we need is a new way
There's something else just a little bit better
It's on the way

NO AUTHORITY

There is someone
who knows everything there is to know
There is someone
who is too afraid to let it show

We live by consequences
We never seem to get it right
Conflict of circumstances
And sometimes we may lose a fight

Wouldn't you know
Something is going wrong
Wouldn't you know
Something is really wrong
You cant do a thing about it

No you have no authority
I am who I want to be

Therc are those of us who
just sit back and never try
There are those of us who
just sit back and wonder why

We live by consequences
We never seem to get it right
Conflict of circumstances
And sometimes we may lose a fight

Wouldn't you know
Something is going wrong
Wouldn't you know
Something is really wrong
You cant do a thing about it

No you have no authority
I am who I want to be

NO WAY OUT BUT THROUGH

You've never been much for the truth
unless its something that you want to use
You waste so much time accepting the lies

I'm not much different than you
We lie to ourselves and we try to make do
Make up your mind and take up a side

There 's no way out but there is a way through

Your building your case with no proof
and filling your head to the rim with a ruse
You waste so much time accepting the lies

A bomb you've got to try and defuse
The longer you wait and the shorter the fuse
Make up your mind and take up a side

There's no way out but there is a way through
you've got nowhere else to go

You can't blame the world for your misfortune
so get up and dust yourself off
Set yourself right

There's no way out but there is a way through
you've got nowhere else to go

NOT ENOUGH

Talk, talk, talk don't talk to me
You've got something I just don't need
Wait, wait, wait, don't wait for me
I've been waiting for you to leave

Want to try and try
Try and make it right
How long it takes you just don't know
And another day
And there's nothing changed
How long it takes you just don't know

Talk, talk, talk don't talk to me
You've got something I just don't need
Wait , wait, wait, don't wait for me
I've been waiting for you to leave

Because we are what we are
and sometimes it's not enough

Try and try, try to make it right
but I just don't know
Another day and there's nothing changed
and I just don't know

Because we are what we are
and sometimes it's not enough

NOT FOR FREE

You want what you think you need
but what you really need
isn't anything that you want

You think that you've got it made
but it's what you don't know
that is gonna pull you down
Down, down, down

It's not for free

You want what you think you need
but what you really need
isn't anything that you want

Stand back, take a step aside
take a look at yourself
put away your stupid pride
It's not for free

NOTHING NEW

There is nothing new put in front of you
Nothing you don't understand
Don't try to rationalize
No one hears your lies
Only you can comprehend

You don't want to see
You don't want to hear
You don't want to feel at all
Tell me that you've tried
Your mind is open wide
but you're not listening at all

Please don't question me I don't have the time
If there's a problem, then it's easier to set aside
There is nothing that will
make you want to change your mind
You can't take it
You can't make it
You can't make it so why try?

There is nothing new put in front of you
Tell me that you've tried
Tell me that your mind is open

Please don't question me I don't have the time
If there's a problem, then it's easier to set aside
There is nothing that will
make you want to change your mind
You can't take it
You can't make it
You can't make it so why try?

NOTHING SUCCEEDS LIKE SUCCESS

My friends are so wrong
They think they know it all
But I know what they're thinking
That I won't make it all of the way
And I won't remember them
it's okay
because I'm going to prove them wrong

Fresh-faced you're the new sensation
Are you happy now?
The voice of a new generation
Congratulations

My friends were so wrong
but I have new friends now
It didn't take me too long to climb my way up here
it's okay
Everyone is showing me the way
They tell me to enjoy my stay

Fresh-faced you're the new sensation
Are you happy now?
The voice of a new generation
Congratulations

Seemed like just yesterday you didn't have a clue
I never thought that this would happen to you

Fresh-faced you're the new sensation
Are you happy now?
The voice of a new generation
Congratulations

NULLIFICATION

So what if I disagree?
Since when did you start listening to me?
So hung up on the way we see
So willing to destroy credibility

We've all got to die of something
So what do we do now?
Right now

Nullification
And we can't stop this any more than you
Nullification
And we can't stop this anymore than you

And what if I disagree?
Then does that make you better than me?
You'll find a way to bury me
Don't underestimate my ability

We've all got to die of something
So what do we do now?
Right now

Nullification
And we can't stop this any more than you
Nullification
And we can't stop this anymore than you

We've all told lies and changed our minds
to justify what they deny

Nullification
And we can't stop this any more than you
Nullification
And we can't stop this anymore than you

ORDINARY

Now you've made it up
it's all inside your mind
Now you've given up
you don't know what's there if you don't try
So you've given in
along with all of your friends
And you're still alone
The means don't always justify the end

Ordinary
Ordinary

A look in the mirror is not enough
What makes you think that you're not one of us?
A look in the mirror is not enough
What makes you think that you're not one of us?

If you make it up
and start to use your mind
It isn't difficult
you don't know what's there if you don't try

Ordinary
Ordinary

A look in the mirror is not enough
What makes you think that you're not one of us?
A look in the mirror is not enough
What makes you think that you're not one of us?

OUT OF FOCUS

I knew what I wanted and I was fixed on it
I was sure of it
I could've been wrong
It seems like it's never quite like I thought it'd be
The reality
am I where I belong?

It's not like they said

It feels like most everything's out of focus in my mind
I'm trying to make some sense out of what I left behind
The difference in who I am and the one want to be
It seemed so much easier
when there was something to believe

A different perspective now and the world I see
is in front of me
and everything's wrong
The grass was much greener when it was next to me
Now it's under me
am I where I belong?

It feels like most everything's out of focus in my mind
I'm trying to make some sense out of what I left behind
The difference in who I am and the one want to be
It seemed so much easier
when there was something to believe

The world
it only seems to change from where you look
Much different than the pictures that they took
It's nothing like they said it would be

It feels like most everything's out of focus in my mind
I'm trying to make some sense out of what I left behind
The difference in who I am and the one want to be
It seemed so much easier
when there was something to believe

"Out of Focus" is from our Reactionary record which was the follow up to the controversial *Ignorance is Bliss*. On the heels of the *Ignorance is Bliss* record we went back into the studio after a brief tour and got back to the drawing board. The thing was we didn't really want to go rushing back into the studio to make a skate punk record. We had just made a very textured, layered album that we labored over and poured ourselves into. So Reactionary wasn't the "return to the roots" album that maybe some people were expecting and in it's time it was seen by most as a stop gap or a place holder which is a shame because I think there are a lot of great songs on the album. We were now writing songs with the experience and knowledge of having made a record like *Ignorance is Bliss* and there was no going back, so while the songs on Reactionary are more pop punk, they still have a kind of sophistication about them.

I feel like the theme of "Out of Focus" is effectively communicated by the title. For me, lyrically, it was a bit of a coming of age song. I had spent most of my youth wishing to have a career writing, recording, and performing music. I felt like I had a plan, a clear goal, and a laser focus. The thing is, as you start working through your plans you can start to have trouble sometimes seeing the forest through the trees. Making records, touring, and the like can become a process in which you develop a myopic focus and if your don't zoom out and change your perspective you can't and won't adjust your goals. I think part of becoming an adult is to be able to determine what your strengths and opportunities are and to maximize them rather than to stick unyieldingly to an arbitrary goal you may have set for yourself without having any real perspective. Dealing with the acceptance and reality of these things is what this song is about.

OVERCOME

Fake
even when you're sure this time it's real
Pain
isn't just defined by what you feel

It isn't so wrong
to be where you're from
The image of what you are
can be overcome

Angst
you'd cut out your heart to spite your mind
Stay
even if it's just a waste of time

It isn't so wrong
To be where you're from
The image of what you are
can be overcome

I let my guard down
I let my guard down
I let my guard down
I let my guard down

PAPER TIGERS WITH TEETH

With the push and shove that's how it's done
Believe it
Better yet from the barrel of a gun
if needed

We can't be everything to everyone
it seems like
this paper tiger's showing teeth

Don't believe the fear and lies
Don't be fooled by your own eyes
They believe the devil is on our side
Don't ignore the rising tide

Incoherent rambling and hate
Believe it
Worlds apart and the hour's getting late
We're bleeding

We can be everything to everyone
it seems like
this paper tiger's showing teeth

Don't believe the fear and lies
Don't be fooled by your own eyes
They believe the devil is on our side
Don't ignore the rising tide

PASTEL

Another falls in place
You wonder if you're only human
It's blood, dust, and paste
We're held together by a single thread
Must be a reason for us to justify it
but no one will deny it

What is it with this place
or is it that I'm missing something?
You won't see my face
when I can't even see it for myself

Must be a reason for us to justify it
but no one will deny it

I don't want a game
that I don't know how to play
just go away
and I don't want to know how to play can't I make it
just go away?

Don't you understand
what these problems will demand?
make it
just go away
I don't want a game
that I don't know how to play
just go away

Must be a reason for us to justify it
but no one will deny it

PERSONA NON GRATA

I know you're not the same
Shouldn't have to take a turn like everybody else
You used to have it made
You never needed anything or anybody else

Really it's all because you're leaning on me
All because you are still not sorry
All because you are never gonna bend
Really it's all because you are breathing on me
All because you are still not sorry
All because it's never gonna end

I won't be the one
to say that you should stop
and take a look inside yourself
I think you're still afraid
to admit that you are really just like everybody else

Really it's all because you're leaning on me
All because you are still not sorry
All because you are never gonna bend
Really it's all because you are breathing on me
All because you are still not sorry
All because it's never gonna end

And I won't make this mistake again
I won't be here to let you in
If I could just get up and walk away
And I'll never play this game again
I want for all of this to end
If I could just get up and walk away

Really it's all because you're leaning on me
All because you are still not sorry
All because you are never gonna bend
Really it's all because you are breathing on me
All because you are still not sorry
All because it's never gonna end

POLISH

garbage in, garbage out

I can't stop this ship from sinking
So full of purpose
So full of meaning
I can't stop this chest from beating
but there's no air here
I'm barely breathing

If I lost control
please protect these things
that I need to be whole
I thought that there'd be more than this
This drowning feeling less and less
And all of the shiny polish on this soul!

garbage in, garbage out

In spite of these best intentions
You don't have to
if you don't want to
Just remember
You're only as good as what you once were
But don't be so sure...

If I lost control
please protect these things
that I need to be whole
I thought that there'd be more than this
This drowning feeling less and less
And all of the shiny polish on this soul!

PRODIGAL

He's never going back
Refuses to be left behind
He doesn't understand
how they so easily made up their minds

You had it in your hands
So how is it so hard to find?
You still don't understand
the reason you've been treated so unkind

There's nowhere left for you to hide
Afraid and bound by your design
If you don't know what you're looking for
what will you find?

You need a little time
so you can get your head around your mind
If you don't know what you're looking for
what will you find?
Something you don't like

You never get it back
So what's the point in killing time?
You still don't understand
the reason you've been treated so unkind

There's nowhere left for you to hide
Afraid and bound by your design
If you don't know what you're looking for
what will you find?

You need a little time
so you can get your head around your mind
If you don't know what you're looking for
what will you find?
Something you don't like

PROMISES

What's the matter with my view?
Is it something less than you think it should be?
What's the matter with the truth?
Is there any of it left for us to see?

That's not the way it is supposed to be
That's not the meaning of equality

I don't want promises
I don't want condescending words from you

You can do most anything
as long as it's exactly how I say
Opportunity is free
Just make sure that you have enough to pay

That's not the way it is supposed to be
That's not the meaning of equality

I don't want promises
I don't want condescending words from you

So go on turn and walk away
I guess there's nothing left to say
I won't make the same mistakes
Can't have it any other way

PROTECTION

I can't understand how we're better off this way
We know the truth still we're trying not to say
what needs to be said in time
I thought I could leave behind
these reasons that made me hide
It's stripping away the disguise

Can you save me from myself?
It's you and no one else
gives me protection

I can't figure out why you're pushing me away
I own the truth so I think I'll be okay

Don't say that I'm in decline
A struggle I can't define
You said I made myself blind
I'm trying to open my eyes

Can you save me from myself?
It's you and no one else gives me protection

You said you'd never be okay
I saw myself in you that day
and I realized everything had changed

Can you save me from myself?
It's you and no one else gives me protection

PUSHOVER

Just like everybody told you
You're a part of what you've done
There's not a single person out there
who isn't carrying a ton around

Your back is nearly breaking
It buckles underneath this weight
They say that everyone gets lucky sometimes
Good to those who wait
But they were wrong

Wrong, wrong
You should be moving on
You've made this victim of yourself
And now they're gone
Gone, gone
You're not where you belong
You've made this victim of yourself

And they were wrong about the weather
They said everything was gray
Another anecdote, I quote
"I guess today's just not your day"

But when tomorrow won't say anything
you'll have to be here now
They said you've taken everything for granted
Buried it somehow
But they were wrong

Wrong, wrong
You should be moving on
You've made this victim of yourself
And now they're gone
Gone, gone
You're not where you belong
You've made this victim of yourself

PUT YOU IN YOUR PLACE

What was that you said to me?
I'm not exactly sure I heard you right
What is it you want from me?
I'm not exactly sure I will comply

You think you've got me where you want
You think you're better
but you're not
I don't mean anything to you
Why?

Don't make me put you in your place
You don't think I'd let you make a fool of me

What do you expect from me?
Are you really looking for a fight?
What do you expect to see?
For me to lose control?
I think I might

You think you've got me where you want
You think you're better
but you're not
I don't mean anything to you
Why?

Don't make me put you in your place
You don't think I'd let you make a fool of me

QUESTIONS STILL REMAIN

When I found out
If I took it as the truth
Could there be another meaning here?
If what you say
is what you wanted to be true
Do you know you've lost your reasoning?

So filled with doubt
So unaffected by the news
I am different than I used to be?
And what you say
I'm so convinced its not the truth
Was it me or was it everything?

But I know that I'm still the same
Everything around me changes
Questions still remain

When I found out
If I took it as the truth
Could there be another meaning here?

If what you say
is what you wanted to be true
Do you know
you've lost your reasoning?

But I know that I'm still the same
Everything around me changes
Questions still remain

RESIGNATION

You can't be right
You're full of prejudice and spite
You think you've got me pegged
but you're wrong

Out of my way
There is a consequence to pay
You think you've got me pegged
but you're wrong

I am someone who'll burn the whole world down
I'm the one to bring it right around

You're giving up on me
but what else have you got?
You're giving up on me

You're losing sight
I won't give up without a fight
You think you've got me pegged
but you're wrong

I'm not afraid
I'll take the chance I have to take
You think you've got me pegged
but you're wrong

I am someone who'll burn the whole world down
I'm the one to bring it right around

You're giving up on me
but what else have you got?
You're giving up on me

You can't expect the world to bend to you
You only feed the fire of anger and our disbelief
I can't be everything to everyone
and I can't be
everything you think that I should be

RIGHT AS RAIN

Right as rain
Right as rain
You just kicked me in the teeth again
Pushed away my only friends
but in the end
we'll still be right as rain

I was behind you
tried like Hell to find you
We were lost
and never wanted to be found

I was so blind then
Left it all behind when
you said you would never kick me to the curb
I'm leaving but I just can't find the words

Right as rain
Right as rain
I'm here beaten up and broken down again

Right as rain
Right as rain
You just kicked me in the teeth again
Pushed away my only friends
but in the end we'll still be right as rain

I'm nothing like you
But I can't deny you
And I feel like
I'm stuck inside looking out

I tried to push back
Got myself on the wrong track

It felt like anything
was easier than this mess
You couldn't care about me any less

Right as rain
Right as rain
I'm here beaten up and broken down again

Right as rain
Right as rain
You just kicked me in the teeth again
Pushed away my only friends
but in the end
we'll still be right as rain

Since you're not with me
A sinking feeling inside of me
I tell myself I'm better off somehow
But I know you'll find me
And someday you'll remind me
Sometimes it's easier
to give up than give in
And you'll be there to meet me
in the end

Right as rain
Right as rain
I'm here beaten up and broken down again

Right as rain
Right as rain
You just kicked me in the teeth again
Pushed away my only friends
but in the end we'll still be right as rain

RUINATION, HERE WE COME!

Your generation's doomed but so is mine
It's worse for you but there may still be time
The world is not only what you define
I realize you think I'm out of line

Why don't we try harder to unite?
Why are we so full of hate and spite?
I guess there's nothing worth the sacrifice
that doesn't add up to their bottom line

Looks like they've won
and ruination here we come
Congratulations
ruination here we come

Save yourself before it's too late

My generation's made mistakes in kind
but we made it possible for you to shine
The world is not only what you define
I don't care if you think I'm out of line

There's not much difference in you and I
I've been around the block a few more times
What's all this boring talk of sacrifice?
Just get some cash and you can pay the price

Look like they've won and ruination here we come
Congratulations ruination here we come

Save yourself before it's too late

RUN IN CIRCLES

You are all the same
Go the way you came
Different names
but very little else has changed

Difficult to find
Easy to resign
Didn't seem to matter
when I didn't mind

Out before it's in
Everybody wins
Give them what they want
and they are giving in

Nothing in return
Will we ever learn?
It's jumbled
and it's getting harder to discern

I run my mind in circles
The vertigo
I've had enough
It feels as though
nothing's going to change

I run my mind in circles
The vertigo
I've had enough
It feels as though
nothing's going to change

SAFETY IS OUR PRIMARY CONCERN

Make way for the execution
Make way for the media whore
Everybody loves an execution

Make time for the explanation
It's mostly lies because the truth is a bore
Everybody's got to have an opinion

And that's great
how we're doing it to ourselves
It's like some kind of game
That we keep trying to tell ourselves
that we're safe
from the danger in our lives
The price we pay

Competition
has its just rewards
Ammunition

High time for an education
A little late on the common sense
They're so effective with intimidation

Make time for the explanation
It's only lies because the truth is a bore
Everybody's got to have an opinion

And that's great
how we're doing it to ourselves
It's like some kind of game
that we keep trying to tell ourselves
that we're safe
from the danger in our lives
The price we pay

While on tour for *face to face*, Scott and I wandered into a music store in Santa Cruz, CA where we saw these really cool baritone guitars. I think we decided on the spot to buy them and to form side project that would only use these baritone guitars. That's how Viva Death started. The song "Safety is Our Primary Concern" is from the eponymous Viva Death debut record. The band would go on to record and release three more full length records. Writing songs for Viva Death was great for me because it was challenging and fun. There were elements of punk rock, but so much more; goth, rock, psychedelica, surf, etc.

This song lyrics are obviously sarcastic (I think), at least the title is. It's a criticism of how our governments, institutions, and corporations lie to us and try and make us think they are benevolent when most of the time in reality human nature drives the individuals in power toward their own self gratification in achieving wealth and power. It is also about how we know this and many times choose to accept it with very little or no push back except for some grumbling and complaining or maybe a strong argument with our friends that ultimately results in nothing. In addition it is about how media is used as a blunt instrument to further the aims of the institutions with power.

As you can see these topics are more akin to what you might expect from typical punk lyrics. Viva Death was a fun way for me to take a break from my real job in *face to face* and to try some new lyrical identities and take some risks. I think the lyrics are more dark in tone and far more gloomy. It was an effective way for me to exercise some demons.

SAY GOODBYE AGAIN

Another lie on lips that say
This might be a mistake
but it's familiar

It doesn't matter anyway
We'd still be heading nowhere
fast

I should've stayed away from you
I almost never do the things
that I'm supposed to do

I should just stay away from you
That's why I don't

And do we get what we deserve?
And if we're satisfied
then what comes after?

You'll never know until you learn
It's a beautiful disaster

I should've stayed away from you
I almost never do the things
that I'm supposed to do

I should just stay away from you
That's why I don't

SAY WHAT YOU WANT

Wise up
You're not the only one
who ever tried to make a difference

Distrust filling up in us
Before we know it truth and lies go hand in glove

Say what you want
Say what you want
I guess I'll see you here tomorrow

Say what you want
Say what you want
Trying to become who they think you should be

See the world through broken glass
A reach that far exceeds the grasp
And here we find ourselves at last
Full of questions we can't ask

Wound up
And now you've had enough
Never mind about tomorrow

Unfun
The thought of waking up
to realize that you were commonly mistaken

Say what you want
Say what you want
I bet I'll see you here tomorrow

Say what you want
Say what you want
Out of time the window's slamming shut on you

See the world through broken glass
A reach that far exceeds the grasp
And here we find ourselves at last
Full of questions we can't ask

Say what you want
Say what you want
Say what you want
Say what you want

SEE IF I CARE

There's nothing left to do here but clean up this mess
I let myself down for the last time
These things that used to matter I couldn't care less

I used to hate being alone
You've taken everything from me I've ever known

I've got nothing left for you
I've got nothing to spare
Whatever it is
you want me to give
Just take it
and see if l care

There's something left to do but I can't lift my head
I told myself this was the last time
I'm really close but I haven't given up yet

I used to hate being alone
You've taken everything from me I've ever known

I've got nothing left for you
I've got nothing to spare
Whatever it is
you want me to give
Just take it
and see if l care

I've done everything for you
I can't break this despair
Whatever it is you need me to give
Just take it
and see if l care

I've got nothing left for you
I've got nothing to spare
Whatever it is you want me to give
Just take it
and see if l care

SELF-DETERMINED

I don't care, you don't care
we aren't going anywhere
Anytime , any place
We're not running in this race

Set yourself apart and be yourself
because you're like no one else
So they say, it's okay
We're all well on our way down

What's standing in the way
keeping us at bay?
Remember what we used to say?

Deafened by the sound
Lift your voice and shout
until there's no one left around
Am I getting somewhere?

I'm afraid that you're afraid
that you might make a big mistake
So here's the point, you missed the point
but I'm okay and you're okay

Set yourself apart and be yourself
because you're like no one else
So they say, it's okay
We're all well on our way down

Deafened by the sound
Lift your voice and shout
until there's no one left around
Am I getting somewhere?

Becoming the cliche
and holding yesterday
so close that we can't break away

SENSIBLE

Someone tell me that I'm wrong
Someone tell me that I'm right
Someone tell me where I'm going
I guess it's safe to say

I don't know what I want
but I can't wait forever
It isn't difficult at all

It makes no sense to me

Someone tell me that it's black
Someone tell me that it's white
Someone tell me that it's going
to make a difference

I don't know what I want
but I can't wait forever
It isn't difficult at all

It makes no sense to me

SHAME ON ME

It started out all wrong
I wasn't thinking
Everything is wrong
I couldn't see it

I guess I thought that things
would somehow try and work themselves out
I'd like to think
it's not so easy to convince myself
that everything is gonna be okay

Shame on me this time
I was only trying to make the best of this
I should have known

Fool me once then shame on you
Again and I must choose between suspicion and naivete
This is what you wanted anyway
This time shame on me

I still believe I'm right
Even though I understand your side
You have your reasons

I guess I thought that things
would somehow try and work themselves out
I'd like to think
it's not so easy to convince myself
that everything is gonna be okay

Shame on me this time
I was only trying to make the best of this
I should have known

Fool me once then shame on you
Again and I must choose between suspicion and naivete
This is what you wanted anyway
This time shame on me

SHINE BOX

Dead on?
disappointing
You're wrong
I'm only halfway come undone
A sting that hasn't stung
but waiting

Go on
suppose me
You can't disappoint me
You've already won
when I was never in you game

And we can't fall down if we don't stand
May the sun shine warm on you face
Until we meet again, God keep you
But there's no room in here to kneel

And there's no reward for good intentions
May the sun shine warm on you face
Until we meet again, God keep you
But there's a path that leads you down

All along
still hoping
There's a chance of destroying
any glimpse of faith
The truth is what we know to be true

And we can't fall down if we don't stand
May the sun shine warm on you face
Until we meet again, God keep you
But there's no room in here to kneel

And there's no reward for good intentions
May the sun shine warm on you face
Until we meet again, God keep you
But there's a path that leads you down

SHOOT THE MOON

Back in ’95 when this was new
I guess I didn’t have a clue
I thought the world would change with the right song

So we picked it up and moved it out
And turned the whole thing upside down
I told myself it wouldn’t be too long

And I believed in everyone
and everything they told me
And I believed that anything
Anything was possible

Shoot the moon
Hit or miss it makes no difference

Back when everything was looking up
I thought I’d never get enough
I didn’t let the world obstruct my view

And we thought that it would never end
We had our fun in spite of it
And paved the way for something slightly new

And I believed in everyone
and everything they told me
And I believed that anything
Anything was possible

Shoot the moon
Hit or miss it makes no difference

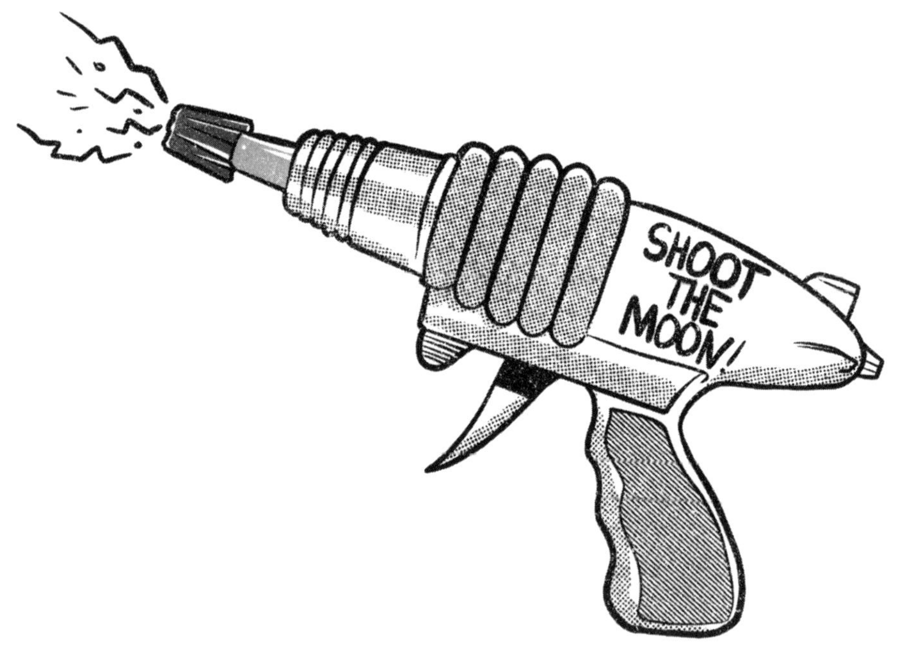
SHOOT THE MOON!

SHOULD ANYTHING GO WRONG

In case of emergency
Break this glass
And pray the alarm makes a sound

The thought is killing me
Out here on my own
and you're nowhere left to be found

I can't explain these memories away

I'm not going to lie to you now
should anything go wrong
There's little that I can do now
should anything go wrong

Please take these things
and don't come try and find me

For your security
Please try and stay calm
Remember what we talked about

I got a hole in me
but I'm not afraid
And neither should you be for now

I can't explain these memories away

I'm not going to lie to you now
should anything go wrong
There's little that I can do
now should anything go wrong

Please take these things
and don't come try and find me

In the early 2000s, *face to face* took a hiatus. We came back together to start playing shows again around 2010 and we also started writing songs again. Our first album after the hiatus was called *Laugh Now, Laugh Later* which was a take on the theater mask themed classic tattoo artwork. The song "Should Anything Go Wrong" is the first song from the album. Because this was a return to form after some years of hiatus, we were genuinely concerned about the direction the songs should take, but in the end I think the record is a good blend of some of our early songwriting style mixed with a fresh, updated version of the music that was inspiring us at the time.

When I started writing lyrics for "Should Anything Go Wrong," I initially came up with the first two lines before I had a title or even a theme for the song. "In case of emergency, break this glass..." I liked this metaphorical theme of how to react to trouble or distress. I think the song is ultimately about fractured relationships that have been so strong that even once they are fractured, there is still a sense of commitment and reliability if one of the other truly need them in a special situation. But it is also a song about how we take things that we keep with us after the relationship is over.

I like the metaphor of pulling the alarm bell as a way to describe a relationship in distress and I wanted to stretch that further to show that the metaphorical alarm doesn't actually work the way you hoped it would. There is a false sense of hope the subject has been relying on for their security and the lyrics reveal that we can't really rely on anything but our own judgement and character.

SICK OF ME

So here I go again
falling headfirst into
this descent
I've tried to shed this skin
but somehow I keep slipping
back into it

Build a wall to stop these demons
Break my bones and I can't feel it
Late again, late again

Shut my eyes to kill these reasons
Boil my blood to keep from healing
Late again, late again

Obligatory grin
Sometimes its too exhausting
to fit in
Why should I pretend
that I need everybody
to be a friend?

Build a wall to stop these demons
Break my bones and I can't feel it
Late again, late again

Shut my eyes to kill these reasons
Boil my blood to keep from healing
Late again, late again

So here I go again
falling headfirst into
this descent
I've tried to shed this skin
but somehow I keep slipping

SMOKESTACKS AND SKYSCRAPERS

We used to live here in glass houses
when we were younger
Eight millimeter black and white
my memories they surrender

Another time in another place
We're never going to go back again
So say goodbye
You're still a little bit homesick
We never seem to find things better than we left them

Tumbling down
crumbling down
Pick up the pieces

Voices of a better vanished time
still echo out there
Smokestacks and skyscrapers
we almost can't remember

Another time in another place
We're never going to go back again
So say goodbye
You're still a little bit homesick
We never seem to find things better than we left them

Tumbling down
crumbling down
Pick up the pieces

Tumbling down
crumbling down
Pick up the pieces

SO LONG

Does your conscience still say anything to you?
You have fallen down so far from what you knew
It's been so long that I
can't believe I still remember
exactly how you used to be

It's not enough
of what you want
you've given up
It's come and gone
Its not enough

You've been running from your shadow in the hall
You've been hanging up your failure on the wall
It's been so long that I
can't believe I still remember
exactly how you used to be

It's not enough
of what you want
you've given up
It's come and gone
It's not enough

SOLITAIRE

I'm not so bulletproof
but this is something
I could never say to you
This sometimes buries me
And I don't know if this is someone I can be

I tell myself it's right
still feels so wrong

It's better than nothing
I'd rather not be here all by myself
It's better than nothing here with someone else

It's better than nothing
I'd rather not be standing here alone
It's better than feeling like you're on your own

I'm not so culpable
I never meant for this to get out of control

I tell myself it's right
still feels so wrong

It's better than nothing
I'd rather not be here all by myself
It's better than nothing here with someone else

It's better than nothing
I'd rather not be standing here alone
It's better than feeling like you're on your own

SPIT SHINE

You know that I know
eventually we'll have to change
There's nothing left and there's nothing
that I want to say

So here we go into the unknown
I should've seen this coming a mile away
You've got to make your own breaks
and I guess that's okay

I'm not so far away it's such a shame

Don't give up without a fight
They're gonna take you for a ride
You better believe there's Hell to pay
But with a little spit shine then you'll be on your way

You know that I know
eventually we'll have to change
There's nothing left and there's nothing
that I want to say

So here we go into the unknown
I should've seen this coming a mile away
You've got to make you're own breaks
and I guess that's okay

I'm not so far away it's such a shame

Don't give up without a fight
They're gonna take you for a ride
You better believe there's Hell to pay
But with a little spit shine then you'll be on your way

STARING BACK

You're wrong!
You're on!
It's like taking candy from a baby and
I don't care
if it hurts because you deserve it

And I
never used to be so happy reveling in grief
The shoe is on the other foot
Now, what's it going to be?

It's all gone
the regrets
And I hate you
but that's still not what I meant
It's okay
To be nothing more than what you are

I never used to be so happy reveling in grief
The shoe is on the other foot
Now, what's it going to be?

You are not going anywhere
You are right back where you started next to me
You are not going anywhere
There is nothing out there anyway
Keep looking but you're staring back at me

STOPGAP

It's not just for me
You should be well a ware of this grief
I know it's temporary
One minute here
the next you're gone like a thief

You got something you wanna say to me?
So what's your story?
better get it straight
Don't waste my time with your apologies
You're afraid
It's an about-face

Atonement isn't for me
It's more pathetic than your sympathy
There's nothing worse than the need
to be accepted to by your contemporaries

You got something you wanna say to me?
So what's your story?
better get it straight
Don't waste my time with your apologies
You're afraid
It's an about-face

Now you're the big shot
you're walking tall
This is a stopgap
you're gonna fall
You deserve what you get
There's no remorse, regret
This is far from over yet
You got something you wanna say to me?

So what's your story?
better get it straight
Don't waste my time with your apologies
You're afraid
It's an about-face

STRUGGLE

There was a hint of danger
They told him it's okay
There was a chance of failure
They told him it's alright
A false security
driven by a weakened state of mind
It's calling and calling

He had a big decision
They told him it's okay
Bound by his indecision
They told him it's alright
Time for reality
Time to gain control of his own life
It's calling and calling

Do you know what is wrong?
Try to keep it in line
You can't go back can't go back
There must be something

He tried
Once was not enough
They told him it's alright
He tried
It wasn't good enough
That doesn't make it right

SYMPTOMATIC

We've got a problem everyone
Do you understand?
Everybody's saying that it's all about them
Everybody's saying they could do without them

War!
We're losing the war
We're losing the war
with every battle that we've won

We've got a disease
Develop a cure
We're treating the symptoms not the cause

You want to know what I'm on about?
Take a look around
Everybody's got to get it all before you
There's no one who would
give a second thought to ignore you

War!
We're losing the war
We're losing the war
with every battle that we've won

We've got a disease
Develop a cure
We're treating the symptoms not the cause

We've got to wake up everyone
and try to figure it out
Some of us are saying that we care about you
Most of us couldn't give a shit about you

War!
We're losing the war
We're losing the war
with every battle that we've won

We've got a disease
Develop a cure
We're treating the symptoms not the cause

We're telling the lies
Destroying the truth
Convincing ourselves that nothing's wrong

We're telling the lies
Inventing the truth
Convincing ourselves that nothing's wrong

War!
We're losing the war
we're losing the war
with every battle that we've won

We've got a disease
develop a cure
We're treating the symptoms not the cause

We're telling the lies
Destroying the truth

Convincing ourselves that nothing's wrong
Convincing ourselves that nothing's wrong
Convincing ourselves that nothing's wrong
Convincing ourselves that nothing's wrong

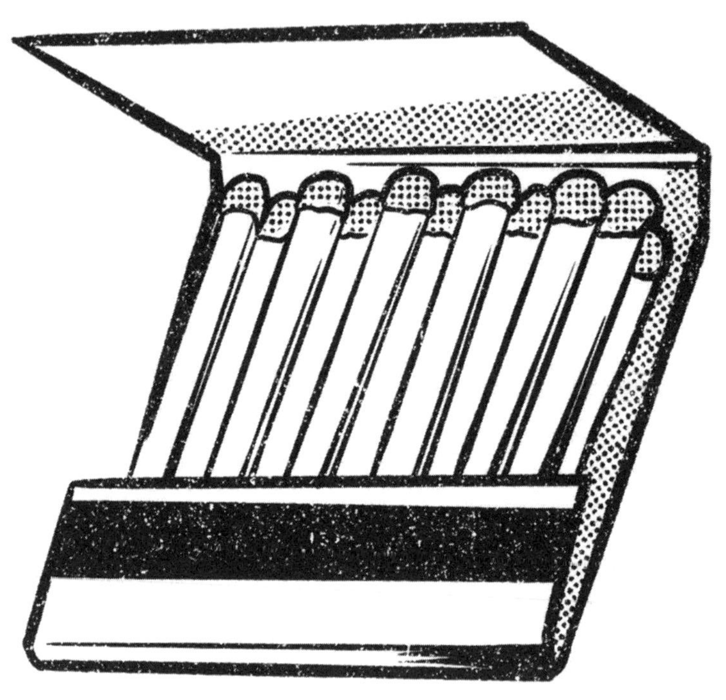

THE TAKE-AWAY

I'm not
what you've sized me up to be inside your head
No way
you could ever see me how I really am

Be careful what you say
because some things never change

It's such a waste of time
but it's so strange
You're only right when something's wrong

You've tried
to give me everything that I could never have
I thought
that you were trying to improve upon yourself

Be careful what you say
because some things never change

It's such a waste of time
but it's so strange
You're only right when something's wrong

Are you ready to do something about it
or is it already too late?
I've given up everything
It hasn't changed a single thing

Are you ready to do something about it
or will you take the easy way?
I can already see you start to disappear
and fade away

I'm not what you've sized me up to be

TAKE IT BACK

I won
I worked too hard to get it
So what?
It's over just forget it

Too much, too soon
Too late until you realize
You've got it made?
You're in for a big surprise!

That's not what I want at all
That's not what I wanted
Can I take it back?
Can I take it back?
I'm asking

It's gone
And I don't want to fake it
It's wrong
I've become the one I hated

Too much, too soon
Too late until you realize
You've got it made?
You're in for a big surprise!

That's not what I want at all
That's not what I wanted
Can I take it back?
Can I take it back?
I'm asking

THICK AS A BRICK

Hooray for annihilation!
Three cheers for the underdogs we are!
Thank you for the inspiration
You think you did it for yourself
but you don't know who you are

Do you think I hate you?
Is it simple as that?
I worked my fingers to the bone
you tied my hands behind my back

How can I make you understand?

Kudos for your new position!
Good luck with the world you now call home
I'll stick with my intuition
You made your mind up
that you know all that there is to know and

Do you think I hate you?
Is it simple as that?
I worked my fingers to the bone
you tied my hands behind my back

How can I make you understand?

THINK FOR YOURSELF

You think you know just what it means
to be alone
You think you've suffered for your cause
you're wrong

I don't really need to know what makes you tick
or what you think is right
I don't want to know the reason you believe

Right now you're like the others
Your thoughts are not your own
Try thinking for yourself
and act on what you know

Still you try to defend these things
you were taught
You've got to try to change the way
you learn

I don't really need to know what makes you tick
or what you think is right
I don't want to know the reason you believe

Right now you're like the others
Your thoughts are not your own
Try thinking for yourself
and act on what you know

Sometimes it feels just like I've burned
every single bridge that I have ever crossed
I always try to learn
from all of these mistakes that I have made

But pride is a worthy adversary
in the struggle for yourself

THIS IS MY VANISHING ACT

I'm not here
this isn't me
I feel as though
I'm watching someone else on this screen

Where am I?
I'm not me
It seems like I was here before
but maybe in a dream?

Please take your seats
We're ready to begin
I promise I won't disappoint
if you stay until the end

Bring the lights down
Try and settle in
Remember it's all make believe
it's really just pretend

I'm alright
let me be
There isn't anything
that you can say to change me

It's gonna be fine just wait and see
I know I shouldn't stay too long
or I risk everything

Please take your seats
We're ready to begin
I promise I won't disappoint
if you stay until the end

Bring the lights down
Try and settle in
Remember it's all make believe
it's really just pretend

THREE CHORDS AND A HALF-TRUTH

Everything I'm telling you is a lie
Everything I'm telling you is a lie

It started off with a white lie
I knew you wouldn't doubt
I can't remember what it was I was lying about
I think it went something like this:
We'll be better off somehow
No more suffering no more pain
No more worry or doubt

You're too hard on yourself
It's not you're fault
You've been played for a fool

With empty heads and empty hands
Nobody gets to choose
There still might be an answer here
Try looking for a different kind of truth

Everything I'm telling you is a lie
Everything I'm telling you is a lie

It started off with a white lie
I knew you wouldn't doubt
I can't remember what it was I was lying about
I think it went something like this:
We'll be better off somehow
No more suffering no more pain
No more worry or doubt

Everything I'm telling you is a lie

TRUTH IN ADVERTISING

Stop what you're doing
and get your story straight
There's talk of chain reaction
and it's heading this way

There's no time to take action
No time for a debate
So just brace yourself and hold on
To whatever they can't break

All we want is just an answer to the question
Are you telling us a lie?

There's a mounting discontent
You can hear it on the air
There's an anger and resentment
You can feel it everywhere

Will you rise to the occasion?
When it comes to your front door
Or will you hide in resignation?
Just the way you did before

All we want is just an answer to the question
Are you telling us a lie?

All we want is just an answer to the question
Are you telling us a lie?

UNCONDITIONAL

Is there a way to become invisible?
You say you might
but you wouldn't dare
I think it works when it's unintentional
I know you hear me
and I know that you don't care
I'm not invisible!

I didn't say that you were unemotional
You put it on like the clothes you wear
You've got emotion but it's one-dimensional
You're full of hate
full of anger
full of fear
I'm not invisible!

No love is unconditional
No way to walk that line
You couldn't make it if you tried

Is there a way to become invisible?
I've done my best to be seen and heard
I'm not amazing and I'm not original
I'm not so sure
did you even catch a word?
I'm not invisible!

No love is unconditional
No way to walk that line
You couldn't make it if you tried

UNDER THE WRECKAGE

I guess I should have listened
to the way you said goodbye
My last remaining thought of you
is only just a lie
I didn't mean to let you leave
but I didn't really try
To keep you here because I didn't
want to answer why

My life
won't mean anything
It's all gone
I lost it all

I keep looking
I can't find you anywhere

So underneath the wreckage
I keep looking for a sign
A way to bring you back to me
there's nothing left to find
There's so much of this mess I made
There's so much I can't hide
I wonder if I found you
could I look you in the eye?

My life
won't mean anything It's all gone
I lost it all

I keep looking
I can't find you anywhere

UNITED BY THE THREAT OF A COMMON ENEMY

I hate you and you hate me
so the only thing we have is that we disagree
I don't know why you don't get it
even some of the time
When it's obvious I'm right
and that's the reason why

You should
look over your shoulder
you smug son of a bitch

I'm laughing out loud
Because I've waited for this moment for such a long time
You need assistance with your resistance?
Well count me in

I'm working on a dish
that's best served cold
So I hope you bring that appetite
for which you're known
I'm not about to jump the gun and make a mistake
So for now I'm going to help you out
but you just wait

Keep your friends close
but keep your enemies closer

I'm laughing out loud
because I've waited for this moment for such a long time
You need assistance with your resistance?
Well count me in

VELOCITY

Tell me something that I don't already know
Tell me how you plan to change the world
I'm tired of people trying to tell me what is right
I'm tired of people trying to pull me down

I know that you might never understand the way I feel
I made a promise to myself that I would never let it show

Never look down
Never look down
Just keep my focus straight ahead
and try to walk this line

Tell me all about your favorite human being
Tell me everything about yourself
God, the story is so terribly interesting!
I wonder what's so good about myself

I know that you might never understand the way I feel
I made a promise to myself that I would never let it show

Never look down
Never look down
Just keep my focus straight ahead
and try to walk this line

So let me take a good look at your perfect life
so I know just exactly how I don't want mine

Never look down
Never look down
Just keep my focus straight ahead
and try to walk this line

VERTIGO-GO

This constant indecision
is gonna be the death of me
I'm lost in self-derision
I know it's not
what's best for me

I've got a nagging feeling
something here is not quite right
Maybe I should just ignore this
it's getting harder
try as I might

'round and 'round the sun we go
easy come
easy go

It feels
like I'm out here on my own
surrounded by a growing inundation of unknown
and fate
is cruel to everyone
but somehow I think I'm the one made an example of

We share a lack of vision
there's nothing clear about the way
with no concern for the collision
we're going out
so come what may

I've got a sinking feeling
no one or thing can make it right
Maybe I should just ignore this
it's getting louder try as I might

’round and ’round the sun we go
easy come
easy go

It feels
like I’m out here on my own
surrounded by a growing inundation of unknown
and fate
is cruel to everyone
but somehow I think I’m the one made an example of

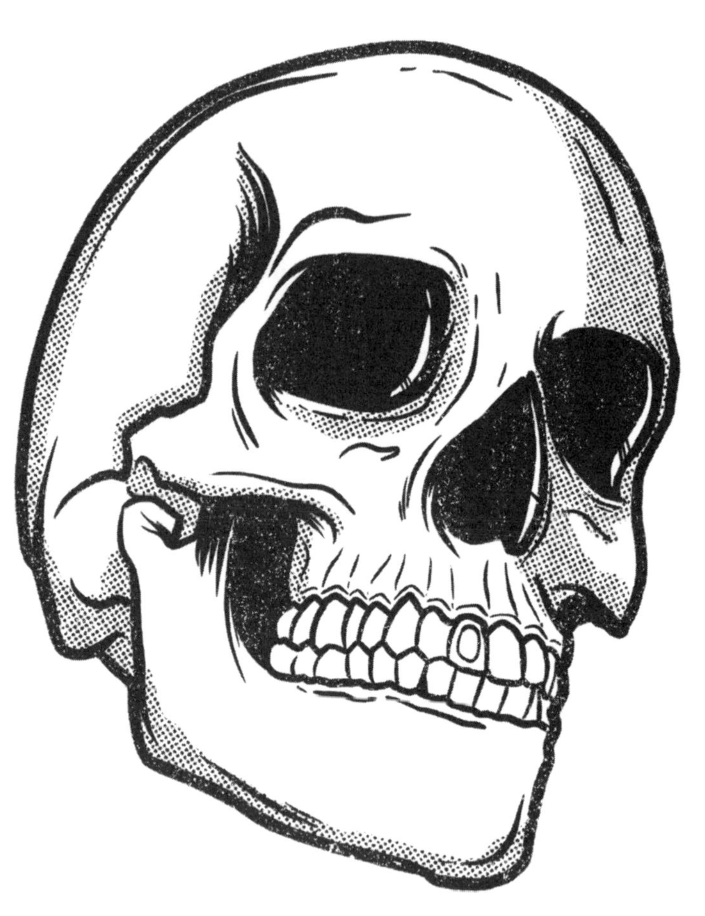

WAITING TO BE SAVED

I heard about this story in the news today
About a man who lost his senses, lost his way
About a man who had his world taken away
He took his life but not before he made them pay

So go on ask yourself the question
Are you convinced that you're okay?
And often times it makes you wonder
Are we not that safe?

I heard a story about this woman yesterday
A twenty-seven year old teacher of fifth grade
A kid brought a gun to school and took her life away
The politicians placed the blame
and nothing changed!

And I feel it today
It feels like nothing else, nothing else
I am waiting to be saved
Helpless!
I feel it today
It feels like nothing else, nothing else
I am waiting to be saved

So go on ask yourself the question
Are you convinced that you're okay?
And often times it makes you wonder
Are we not that safe?

And I feel it today
It feels like nothing else, nothing else
I am waiting to be saved
Helpless!
I feel it today
It feels like nothing else, nothing else
I am waiting to be saved

WAKE UP

You don't understand because you won't
Looks like this time you're on your own

I know there's something else that's eating you
and I'm afraid its something I won't do
Because it's not like the last time
but this is the last time
I'm through

Wake up, wake up
lift those heavy eyes
Get up, wake up
time to rise and shine

You didn't believe me
no surprise
an eternity
but I got wise

I know there's something else that's eating you
and I'm afraid its something I won't do
Because it's not like the last time
but this is the last time
I'm through

Wake up, wake up
lift those heavy eyes
Get up, wake up
time to rise and shine

I know there's something else that's eating you
and I'm afraid its something I won't do
Because it's not like the last time
but this is the last time
I'm through

Wake up, wake up
you've worn out your welcome here
Get up, wake up
Go on and disappear

WALK AWAY

Don't want to hear what you said
Don't want to kick in your head
Don't want to live my life that way

Don't want to give in but I
Don't want to be victimized
Don't want to live my life that way

Walk away
Try to see things in a different way

Don't want to tell you your place
Don't want to get in your face
Don't want to live my life that way

Don't want to know what you think
Don't want to know anything
Don't want to live my life that way

Walk away
Try to see things in a different way

WALK THE WALK

I could be like you
I could be alone and jaded
Wondering what to do until they say
And I could be like you
angry and intoxicated
Wondering what to do to make them pay

Will I find a way?
Can I make them see?
And make them all believe you're wrong
You're really wrong
Your ill intentions don't belong

I hear you talk the talk
but I don't see you walk the walk
and I still don't believe a thing you say

I could be like you
I could be alone and jaded
Wondering what to do until they say

Will I find a way?
Can I make them see?
And make them all believe you're wrong
You're really wrong
Your ill intentions don't belong

I hear you talk the talk
but I don't see you walk the walk
and I still don't believe a thing you say

WELCOME BACK TO NOTHING

I'll be the one you love
I'll be the one you love to hate
No way you're going back
Waited too long now it's too late

Don't call it desperation
You're circling the drain
Just a minor set back
You'll ignore the pain

You were supposed to be the golden one
You're going out to shine tonight
Welcome back to nothing

I'll take you by the hand
I'll take your hand and I will bite
Your tail's between your legs
You're really giving up so quick this time?

It smacks of desperation
You're circling the drain
Set back after set back
It's misery and pain

They said you were the chosen one
You're going out to shine tonight
Welcome back to nothing

WHAT'S IN A NAME?

Open-minded educated
Popular and medicated now
And you still won't make it
Filled with silent indignation
Blind with hopeless expectation now
And you still won't make it

So you're afraid that they will think ill of you
Get a load of me now
And if you're scared they couldn't care less of you
Get over yourself now

It's fame and popularity
I'll never understand
If it feels like this is what you need
You'll never understand

Innocence and innuendo
Confidence and acquiescence now
And you still won't make it
Self-consciousness is not a virtue
Everyone is looking at you now
You may never make it

So you're afraid that they will think ill of you
Get a load of me now
And if you're scared they couldn't care less of you
Get over yourself now

WHAT YOU CAME FOR

And I don't know
if what you came for is still around
And I don't know
if what you came for is still around

And please don't leave
And please don't leave

It's not what I've been looking for
but you showed me there's something more
than I could ever see inside myself
When you left me here I fell apart
In spite of you and in spite of myself

And I don't know
if what you came for is still around
And I don't know
if what you came for is still around

And please don't leave
And please don't leave

It's not what I've been looking for
but you showed me there's something more
than I could ever see inside myself
When you left me here I fell apart
In spite of you and in spite of myself

WHY WOULD I LIE?

I've been involved and I've paid attention
I've listened to every word you've said
You tell a lie and I fake my interest

I was around when it really happened
From the beginning until the end
So what's the point of an explanation?

Why would I lie?
Is there anything I left from my story?
This type of deception would be
a waste of both of our time

You start to trust as you dull your instincts
I've tried my best but I still don't care
You've opened up to a disappointment

I know my way around this conversation
You've had enough but you're standing there
I leave it up to interpretation

Why would I lie?
Is there anything I left from my story?
This type of deception would be
a waste of both of our time

Maybe there's a chance
that everything is going to work out for the best
Maybe there's a chance
that pigs will grow wings and fly

Why would I lie?
Is there anything I left from my story?
This type of deception would be
a waste of both of our time

THE WORLD IN FRONT OF YOU

Stopped the fighting
you don't care at all
Gave up trying
you don't care at all
Something's dying
you don't care at all
Sick of crying
you don't care at all

Here we go
Lining up taking sides
Waiting so long
Too ashamed
too much pride

Will unbending
you don't care at all
No one's listening
you don't care at all
Something's missing
you don't care at all
Stop pretending
you don't care at all

Here we go
Lining up taking sides
Waiting so long
Too ashamed
too much pride

I was hoping for a chain reaction
I was waiting for the satisfaction
You were nothing but a brief distraction
I can't see the world in front of you

YOU COULD'VE HAD EVERYTHING

Ignorance and arrogance mean quite the same to me
Take a look around you and I'm sure you will agree

The world is full of people filled with hatred,
filled with greed
It's such a rare example w
hen you've found a human being

You could've had everything, but you
You would've been scared of what to do
You should've been so much more to us
than just exonerated
Why shouldn't it break your heart in two?

I find little entertains me anymore
The problems of the world are often tedious and worn

I'm reading all about it with a chuckle and a sneer
They say a new beginning and they say the end is near

You could've had everything, but you
You would've been scared of what to do
You should've been so much more to us
than just exonerated
Why shouldn't it break your heart in two?

Get in your self-assuredness and take it for a spin
You'll be standing by yourself when they've all given in

It's take before it's taken from you every single day
I wish it wasn't like this I don't know another way

You could've had everything, but you
You would've been scared of what to do

You should've been so much more to us
than just exonerated
Why shouldn't it break your heart in two?

YOU LIED

There's nothing here
inside of these walls
I feel like I am so far away
Nothing's changed and I just can't be
who I'm supposed to be

I let the past control my life
it brings me to my knees and I can not hide
I cannot lie

So many words to say and no one to hear
Why did you go away?
I needed you more today than I ever did
You lied to me

Outside it's cold
It chills to the bone
I wish that I did not have to see

I let the past control my life
It brings me to my knees and I can not hide
I cannot lie

So many words to say and no one to hear
Why did you go away?
I needed you more today than I ever did
You lied to me

YOU'VE DONE NOTHING

You don't know what you want to be
You don't know what you want to do
Never going to amount to much of anything
So what's the difference if you win or lose?

Well that's something
Well isn't that something?

You've done nothing wrong
and it's never your fault
You've done nothing

You don't care where your friends have gone
because you never really needed them anyway
Never going to be exactly who you are
because you try too hard to be just like them

Well that's something
Well isn't that something?

You've done nothing wrong
and it's never your fault
You've done nothing

YOU'VE GOT A PROBLEM

So what's the problem now this time?
I thought you'd learn by now
that nothing ever works out right
You want to take away the edge
You tell me it's the only thing
that helps you forget

You've made your promises
That's not enough this time
There's only so much you can squander
from a feeble mind

You've got a problem with your life

You've got a problem with your mind
Don't try to tell me that you
think it's going to work out fine
So go ahead and try to hide
The world around you watches on
as you destroy your life

Do what your problem says
There's not a lot of time
There's only so much you can squander
from a feeble mind

You've got a problem with your life

YOU WERE WRONG ABOUT ME

There's something wrong with me
There's something wrong with me
There's something wrong with my head

Don't wait too long for me
Don't wait too long for me
Don't wait too long no regrets

It's give and take and take and take
and give until its gone

I'm still standing here
I never backed down let's be clear
you were wrong

I don't belong in here
I don't belong in here
I don't belong in my head

There's nothing wrong with me
There's nothing wrong with me
There's nothing wrong with me yet

It's give and take and take and take
and give until its gone

I'm still standing here I never backed down let's be clear
you were wrong